LINES OF A LAYMAN

LINES OF A LAYMAN

J. C. PENNEY

 CHANNEL PRESS   GREAT NECK · NEW YORK

Table of Contents

II IN OUR DAILY TASKS, 77

Foreword

Lines of a Layman, by Mr. J. C. Penney, has been for nearly a generation one of the most popular features of *Christian Herald Magazine*—and increasingly popular it is. These characteristic, scintillating and often profoundly moving lay sermonettes are now yours in a volume which, we believe, will become a bestseller in its field.

Mr. Penney is today the most distinguished merchant prince of our time. He lives and moves—and how he does move—in the tradition of John Wanamaker. And even the career of John Wanamaker was not more versatile and many-sided than is that of the author of *Lines of a Layman*. From his "Six Principles of Daily Living" through his "Four-square Men," his "Faith of Personal Experience," his chapter on family and young people, his vivid personal reminiscences, his "Christian and the Social Order," his eloquent "The American Way"—these chapters, with their many facets which include religion, patriotism, human relationships, social adjustments and sound advice for getting on in business and industry, lead to such conclusions as this: " 'What shall it profit a man if he gain the whole world and lose his own soul?' . . . That question is for nations as well as for individuals. Neither men nor nations can live by physical bread alone."

Mr. Penney's own rich and poignant experience, which led him deep into pain, sorrow and disillusionment, but out of the darkness at last into full light of radiant Christian achievement, proves the validity of that conclusion.

Today, when practically all men of his years would be in retirement, this man is living more vigorously than in any period of his life before. He continues to travel the continent and world. As I write these lines, he is with Mrs. Penney in India, visiting a daughter. His schedule calls for an extended journey to the Far East, including Formosa where his youngest son resides. He is the active Chairman of the Board of the company he founded more than half a century ago.

Beginning in the pioneer town of Kemmer in western Wyoming, the organization which proudly bears his name has expanded into one of the few billion-dollar enterprises of America. His interests are multiple. He is the President of a distinguished enterprise of Christian laymen; President of the Friends of the Chapel of Four Chaplains, the unique Interfaith Memorial at the heart of Temple University in Philadelphia; Chairman of the Board of Trustees of Allied Youth, Inc., perhaps the most remarkable high school activity on this continent (the character of the program is distinguished by one of its slogans, "Fun Without Alcohol"). But it would be quite impossible to enumerate the many fields in which this remarkable man continues to release his life.

Recently, when his family, neighbors and his friends from all over America gathered to celebrate his 80th anniversary, he was the life of the party. More than 500 were present, and that occasion was in all respects characteristic of the man. It, too, was "fun without alcohol."

My association with the versatile author of these "Lines" reaches back into the years for considerably more than a quarter of a century. I have watched him grow in breadth of vision and versatility of speech and writing, and I believe that on these pages, as nowhere else, you will find the measure of the man.

—DANIEL A. POLING

I

LESSONS FOR EVERYDAY LIVING

Four-square Man

THIS SUBJECT IS the one nearest my heart. It is unfortunate that so many men go through life in just the ordinary way. Many are inclined to think that only geniuses, or men with special privileges, succeed. To my way of thinking, success is but a result of which the four-square man is the cause. But in order to be a four-square man, one must possess the essential qualities, the first of which I should say is *purpose*.

In other words, a man must have a vision. A man of vision is a man of imagination. Imagination is the power back of initiative. The individual without the fully-developed imaginative faculty is certain to get into a rut. It is this quality in man which has lifted us from the plane of the savage to our present degree of civilization.

Contemplate the developments in science, art, literature, religion, and inventions during the last century. Think of what the railroads have done for this country. Consider what electricity has accomplished; what the developments in agriculture, mining and irrigation have achieved. These inventions and developments were not the result of chance, but the outcome of someone's thought, the fruits of constructive imagination and purpose.

Now, think of man in his primitive state, dwelling in caves, subsisting on roots, clothing himself from the skins of animals.

What a change in a few hundred years and what an incentive for us to use our powers of constructive imagination!

An objective is necessary. Yet, how many men are drifting, are human derelicts floating on the sea of life with no objective in view.

The mind, feelings and the physical body are Divine gifts, and the man who fails to make use of these gifts is the man of no purpose.

The second essential quality in the four-square man is that of *integrity*. The word is derived from the Latin *integer*, meaning whole. Hence, an honest man is a whole man, not a fraction of a man. He is not one thing above the line and something else below it; not one thing at home and something else away from home; but a whole man.

I do not mean to apply this to the handling of money alone. Some men think that so long as they can get by, or keep out of jail, they are honest. A man of integrity is a man of sterling character: one whose word is as good as his bond; who would not think of taking a minute of time that did not belong to him; a man honest with himself. Franklin and Lincoln were such men, men whose names are immortal and whose lives are an inspiration to thousands of others.

My father used to say that he never aspired to be rich, but he wished that when life was over, people in passing his grave might say: "Here lies an honest man." This statement has had tremendous influence on my life.

The moral grandeur of independent integrity is the sublimest thing in nature; so if a man is a man of integrity, and of purpose, he is well on his way to being the four-square man.

Even though the four-square man possesses purpose and integrity, these qualities are of little use if he is not a man of *service*.

Service is coming to be one of the biggest words in the English language. Life's greatest pleasure and satisfaction is found in giving; and the greatest gift of all gifts is that of one's self. You cannot render service if you are selfish or jealous, or not willing to sacrifice. How we admire the individual who is thoroughly unselfish, who thinks of the other fellow before he thinks of himself. How much more pleasure the man gets out of life who "gives before he gets."

Very often someone says, "What's the use? People do not remember what you have done after one is dead and gone."

Do you think I shall ever forget my father? Didn't your mother stint in order that you might have advantages which you could not otherwise have enjoyed? My parents did, and I shall never forget the many sacrifices they made for their children.

The fourth side of the square has to do with a man's soul, and for that reason it is the most important of all. In reality these bodies of ours are leased to us for a term of years. We should so live that it may be said of us, "The world is better for his having lived."

Such an individual is in tune with the Infinite. He is not only happy, but he makes others happy. He has faith in God and love for his fellow man. He is charitable, which enables him to see the good in folks. Just as each member of an orchestra will tune to a certain pitch before playing, so a man each day should tune to the Infinite in order that his ideals may be high and right.

A good motto to follow is found in the words of Henry Van Dyke:

> "Be a breeze from the mountain height;
> Be a fountain of pure delight;
> Be a star serene, shining clear and keen
> Through the darkness and dread of the night;
> Be something Holy and helpful and bright;
> Be the best that you can with all your might."

Prayer As A Way Of Life

IN DISCUSSING PRAYER, you and I need to remember that our actions should conform to the spirit of our prayers. "To pray on rising and then to behave the rest of the day like a pagan is absurd." None of us wants to be guilty of this. To avoid the possibility we need to pray all through the day. The suggestion of one is, "Very brief thoughts, mental invocations can hold a man in the presence of God. All conduct is then inspired by prayer. Thus when prayer is so understood, it becomes a way of life."

This would not deny the value of a set time for prayer. Some would go so far as to urge the value of a specific place. For some time now I have found the spending of fifteen to thirty minutes each day just before retiring in reading and prayer to be exceedingly helpful—so much so that I would not let the day go by without this practice. I read from one or more of several books which I have found helpful. In this way my last thoughts before going to sleep are on God, on Christ, on my spiritual needs and those of others. Such a plan may not work for you. But human nature being what it is, I sincerely believe some plan is needed for each of us, and that as we grow, it will be adjusted to meet our spiritual needs. "Every technique of prayer is good which draws man nearer to God."

The Privilege Of Loving God

THERE IS AN element in the practice of prayer which we men especially are reluctant to consider because it appears to be a feminine characteristic. That is love. Yet those who write with authority on prayer insist that if we can arouse love in the hearts of men, we will not need to spend time trying to convince them that they must pray—both for themselves and for their neighbors.

A basic law in religion is devotion to our God. Jesus shows this perfectly in His devotion to God, from Whom He was never separated. If we must love God as sincerely as we do the person dearest to us, how can we do it? Perhaps it will help us if we first recognize the privilege we have of loving God. Let us remind ourselves that a full understanding of life is impossible without love for God. We should try spending some time each day recalling His goodness, our dependence, and finally offering gifts to Him, such as an act of self-denial, an act of kindness to one in need but done in His name.

As for loving our fellow man, we are conditioned against this. By custom real affection is reserved for the few members of our immediate family and an occasional friend. But such is less than what Christ taught. A man will not carry his share of responsibility for sustaining a brotherhood of men if he does not at the same time love God. Neither can he love God if he does not have real affection for his fellow man.

To Succeed, Win Man's Respect

IF YOU want to do well by yourSELF, if you want to make a
place for yourself in this world, win the respect of those with
whom you come in contact; don't overlook what the Golden
Rule philosophy can do for you. Bread cast upon the waters
returns to you manyfold.

What I have said applies to your dealings with human beings in every walk of life. It applies to your friends, to your
business associates. It applies to the driver of the bus who
takes you to work, to the girl behind the counter who sells
you something you need. And it applies to people of every
race, nationality and faith. As the prophet Malachi said:
"Have we not one Father? Hath not one God created us?"

This would be a good thing to keep in mind in our daily
rounds, to remind us that all of us are the children of God,
those children to whom the great Teacher said: "A new com-
mandment I give unto you, that ye love one another."

I did not mean to make this sound quite so much like a
preachment, but I did want to share with you some of the
conclusions I have come to from many, many years of dealing with people. If you are fortunate, as I was, you learn
sooner or later that you cannot live quite successfully without faith in God and in His creations. I hope I have helped a
little to convince you of this, and to share with you what I
earnestly believe to be a formula for successful and contented
living.

And He Said Unto Them

"The Sabbath was made for man,
and not man for the Sabbath."

PROBABLY NO SAYING of the Master Teacher has been made use of more flippantly than the above. The rules of the Scribes enumerated thirty-nine kinds of work forbidden on the Sabbath. Jesus' disciples, for example, who plucked ears of corn in passing through a field on the Sabbath, had violated that one of the thirty-nine rules which forbade harvesting. And in healing the sick, Jesus Himself broke the rule that a sick man should not receive medical aid on the Sabbath unless his life was in danger. I doubt that any other of the Ten Commandments has been the subject of so much legislation, such heated controversies, as that pertaining to the Sabbath.

I believe in a strict observance of Sunday. I believe that every man owes it to himself, his family, his community and his country, not only to refrain from labor on Sunday, but to interest himself in the religious exercises conducted on that day. I believe that a man becomes a better man than he otherwise would be by attending some church, the one institution having for its field of endeavor the worship of God, and the combating of all manner of sinister, corrupting and debauching influences.

A man in any walk of life who conscientiously observes the Sabbath by taking advantage of the inspirational and tranquilizing influences of such observance, is made stronger physically, mentally and spiritually.

Our Spiritual Heritage And Obligations

I HAVE found silence to be a powerful element in prayer. To learn to be alone with God even in the presence of others is something we Christian laymen should try to do. There are innumerable times during the day when we can turn our thoughts, even for a moment, from business affairs and center them on God's goodness, Christ's love, our fellow man's needs.

I have not omitted by design reference to our obligation as laymen to the church. Rich is our spiritual heritage, and we all owe more to the church than we can ever repay for preserving Christ's teachings, holding together believers, providing a place for religious instruction for ourselves and our children, and giving spiritual leadership in our home communities, our nation and the world. The layman should give himself, his talents, his experience and support to the church. The church in turn should offer an even greater opportunity for spiritual growth to the layman. It should help him see the necessity of bridging the gap between the practical and the spiritual, and then counsel him as he proceeds to take the steps day by day which will result in spiritualizing all of his daily contacts.

The Boy Who Believed

AUGUSTE JOHANIK, a fifteen-year-old boy, went with his parents to settle in Wisconsin in 1909. They were desperately poor. Seventy-five dollars—all they had—was invested in forty acres of stump land.

A heartbreaking struggle commenced to turn this waste into a farm. The father was more than sixty years old. Auguste went to work in a lumber camp at a dollar a day to get enough money to buy food. Two years they toiled, reclaiming their acres from the stumps, building a little house, and accumulating a few implements.

Then a forest fire swept everything away. Homeless and penniless, they stood on their blackened acres. They started in again, at the bottom. Once more they put their little farm in working order.

Auguste had become the head of the family, by 1912, and had obtained two cows. Gradually a herd was developed. Then disease practically wiped him out. But the boy pressed his lips more tightly together. And once more he suffered disaster, but still he refused to recognize defeat.

At last he seemed on the way to success. Again he had a herd of fine cows; and then, for a second time, fire swept over his clearing. "Thank the Lord," said Mr. Johanik, "I have enough insurance to start a foundation." And, giving his praise for this blessing, he rebuilt.

Now he was deeply in debt. Taxes were high and he strained every nerve to meet the interest on his notes.

He was not satisfied with inferior cattle. He fought for the best, insisting that some day the best would enable him to buy food and clothes and a few of the comforts of life.

Was his faith justified? It was. In 1926 he took his most beautiful Guernsey cow, Mary's Pride, to a national sale in Chicago. He hoped she might sell for five hundred dollars and ease the load of his debts. To his astonishment the purchase price was more than two thousand dollars! The sum fairly stunned the owner. It meant relief from poverty; it meant that now there could be flour in the barrel of the kitchen and feed in the bin of the stable at the same time. Said Mr. Johanik, "I must admit that I cried." And who can blame him!

And what shall we say of ourselves, we who have been discouraged with much less of a struggle?

A Cheerful Giver

GOD LOVETH a cheerful giver, not only one who gives money, but one who gives of self. Such a man has something more in mind than the mere making of money. His individuality and his high ideals find expression. Such a man is not only rendering a greater service on this earth, but he is preparing himself for a richer, fuller life to come.

Influence

DID YOU EVER stop to consider that your every thought, word
and action has a direct influence, not only on your own life,
but on that of the people associated with you? Nor is our
influence always confined to our immediate associates. This
lesson I learned from a tree as its branches swung to and
fro upon the wall. Our "shadow-selves" may reach where we
may never go. A man's influence is immortal. Why then not
strive to make its perpetuation worth-while?

A man of influence is a man of character and honesty. Let
each one, therefore, realize the opportunity he has to be a
force in his community.

You will find that a great opportunity is literally locked up
in the spare moments of life. A little effort in reading and
study will occupy your spare time and prepare you for future
work. Rest, when you must, with a purpose. In short, turn
work, time and experience to the best account.

I find that the men who have played a peculiar part in my
career have been those who have directed my mind toward
constructive thinking.

The Material And Spiritual Selves

MR. GLADSTONE used to take great delight in asking his favorite conundrum. It was this: What is everybody in the world doing all the time? And the answer which pleased the grand old man so much was this: Growing older.

Now the average man as he grows older becomes more satisfied and solidified. He gets fixed in his habits and very soon he finds he cannot change. That man is a material and a spiritual being.

Now, we must get these two of us in right relation. The spiritual man in us is the eternal enduring, creating self to live and progress forever. The Father of us all so wills it.

The material self of us, hard to manage, disobedient, illogical, chasing false gods and unworthy companions, should be the servant of the spiritual self, and should work obediently for it.

Good Judgment

JUDGMENT IS DEFINED by Webster as the mental act of judging: the operation of the mind involving comparison and discrimination by which knowledge of the value and relation of things, whether of moral qualities, intellectual concepts, logical propositions or material facts, is mentally asserted or formulated.

To be able to discriminate justly and wisely, to decide without fear or favor, is a quality to be admired in any man. Such a man is eagerly sought in all activities of life. It is not always easy to be unbiased, for as human nature is much the same in us all, we allow our judgment to be colored by that which affects us most. However, there are men big enough to forget their own interests and render decisions in favor of the greatest good to the greatest number. Such men are in the minority, but they stand head and shoulders above their fellow men; consequently they are easily distinguishable.

A man's judgment is usually based on the sum total of his experiences. That is why a man with a practical education so often makes a successful business man; his judgments result from practical experience and not from theory. I am not depreciating, however, the value of a college education. Theory is splendid, but until put into practice, it is valueless.

We are forming judgments every day of our lives. The result perhaps will be unknown for some time. But if we live clean lives, think only clean thoughts, have a purpose in life, remain obedient to God, to our neighbors and ourselves; if we are industrious, decide fairly and justly, then we shall unconsciously form character that will endure.

In life there often arises a situation resembling the forks of a road. We are called upon to choose in which direction we shall travel. If we have decided where we want to go, and are not particular whether the road be rough or smooth, long or short, we shall finally arrive at our destinations. But if we simply take the road that looks easy and attractive, it may lead us to places other than where we wanted to go.

Service Is Unselfish

TOO MANY MEN ask, "What is there in this thing for me?" The service they are willing to render is in proportion to the remuneration they expect to receive. A real man who renders service regardless of his wage is a valuable asset to any community.

The men who have furnished me with my greatest inspiration have not been men of wealth, but men of deeds. Service cannot be bought or paid for in money. It must be earned and rendered.

The Spirit Of Confidence

WHILE WAITING for a train one evening, I overheard a man saying: "He thinks he is the whole thing about our office, but I'll show him before long who has the ability to do things." The facial expression and the movement of hands and head were even more revealing of the man's disposition than his words. Something was wrong with his heart, and its poison was influencing his mind.

Honest rivalry is a fine thing, but the difficulty is to keep it honest. Rivalry intensified frequently results in jealousy that will destroy the nobler virtues of life, if it is permitted to grow. It requires big men not to become bitter in rivalry.

Some folks are not jealous. Their situation in life precludes such an undesirable experience. Others seem to be born with the jealous tendency bulking large in their natures. It seems to grow without special cultivation.

Jealousy should be resisted, throttled and overcome. The ordeal may not be pleasant, but it is necessary. The moment we are jealous, we begin to fall behind in the race. Let us use the powers of our minds and souls for constructive purposes, rather than permit them to burn up in profligate passion. Let us mind our own affairs with fidelity, cultivate a spirit of confidence in others and note how the fruits of friendship ripen into mutual happiness.

Building Upon Experience

EXPERIENCE IS THE great teacher. I shall never forget the remark an uncle made to me one time when I was a small lad. "My boy," said he, "you will have to breathe it through your own nose."

I could hardly grasp the significance of his remark, but I never forgot it, and I think frequently of it now. One cannot give experience to another; it must be acquired by the individual himself.

Experience, when backed by good judgment, is bound to produce results. Many times, however, conditions arise in a man's life for which he has no precedent. It is then that a man, by reason of his experience, is able to look into the future and decide wisely. It was Patrick Henry who said that he had but one lamp by which he was guided, and that was the Lamp of Experience.

Sowing And Reaping

MEN ARE LEARNING more every day that the Bible is a good
text-book, and that it contains the fundamental principles
upon which all business laws are based.

"As ye sow so shall ye reap" is as true in business as it is in
anything else. "Cast ye not good seed on stony ground." Certainly, business men can fully appreciate this injunction.

Harvest is the result of much effort. If it is to be bountiful,
the soil must be well prepared, the seed selected with care,
the ground thoroughly cultivated, and the weeds not allowed
to grow. Then, if the harvest—on which so much depends—is
not taken at the proper time, a great loss is entailed.

In our thought and actions today we are sowing seed. What
shall the harvest be? The ne'er-do-well is apt to regard success as a matter of luck, and naturally looks upon himself as
one of the unfortunate ones. But a successful man realizes
that it is not a matter of luck, but of sowing the proper seed
at the proper time, watching closely the period of cultivation,
and taking care of the harvest.

A man in business sows and reaps just as surely as does the
farmer. The storeman selects a town in which to do business.
He stocks his store with merchandise suited to the needs of
his locality and the trade to which he will cater. If the merchant uses good judgment, if he has been careful in the
choosing of assistants, then the harvest is likely to be boun-

teous. But if he has failed in any of these efforts, his preparations will be as seed cast upon stony ground. We have learned that "from thorns we cannot gather grapes, nor figs from thistles."

Pluck

OFTEN WE HEAR people say of a successful man, "He is a genius," or "He is lucky." The fact is, as someone aptly said, genius is only a capacity for hard work. Luck should be P-L-U-C-K. It will get one farther.

There are, of course, extraordinary men and women, just as there are giants; but though giants are few, they are still human beings. So it is with genius. What we usually call genius is nothing more than common horse sense and a willingness to work, backed up by energy and determination.

Obedience

OBEDIENCE IS RESPECT for authority. It does not necessarily mean submission, but rather cooperation. As children we are taught to obey our parents. Obedience builds us in strength, integrity and right viewpoint.

Indulgence by parents has ruined many children. I know of a man whose wealthy father established him in business three times, but the son made a failure of it each time. Had anyone looked back over the boy's lifetime, it would have been evident that disobedience, lack of respect for authority in home and school, disregard of the teachings of parents and teacher, had pointed the way to this failure in adult life. He continued to fail until voluntarily he grasped the great principle of obedience. But the fact is, he has never yet grasped it fully; and today, though past fifty years of age, he is working for a small salary.

A man does not have the ability to make the proper use of funds given him unless he has had careful, strict training during his formative years.

Force Of Early Experience

OUR EXPERIENCES OF childhood days are much more deeply impressed upon the mind than the events of yesterday. For that reason, too much stress cannot be laid upon the necessity of a careful and early training for our boys and girls. The experiences which come to them in their homes and in school life very often determine their future.

Business is a school, and experience is the teacher. Each individual is the student. Every day of our lives we have new experiences and our success in life depends on how well we apply the lessons learned from experience.

A man may spend years of his life acquiring knowledge, but unless he puts it to some good use as he gathers it, his learning is of little avail.

Six Principles For Daily Living

THERE ARE SIX searching principles that I have adopted for my daily living. I believe they are the essentials of success.

I believe that preparation wins. A man must know all about his business; he must know a little more than any other man knows. As a rule we achieve what we prepare for.

I believe that hard work wins. The only kind of luck that any man is justified in banking on is hard work, which is made up of sacrifice, persistent effort, and dogged determination. Growth is never by mere chance.

I believe that honesty wins. Not only the kind of honesty that keeps a man's fingers out of his neighbor's till, but the finer honesty that will not allow a man to give less than his best, the kind of honesty that makes him count not his hours but his duties and opportunities.

I believe that confidence in men wins. I have found my most successful associates by giving men responsibility, by making them feel that I relied upon them; and those who have proved to be unworthy have only caused the others, who far outnumbered them, to stand in a clearer light.

I believe that the spirit wins. One of the wisest men who ever lived said, "The letter killeth, the spirit giveth life." Every enterprise I have been interested in demonstrates this fact. It is the spirit of the individuals comprising any organization, the spirit of the pioneers in any enterprise or endeavor that will conquer all difficulties and achieve success.

I believe in a practical application of the Golden Rule, as enunciated by the Master Teacher on the hillsides of Judea nearly two thousand years ago. "Therefore all things whatsoever ye would that men should do to you, do ye even so to them: for this is the law and the prophets."

Empty Lives

TOO MANY MEN close their purse strings and cut their heart strings—and so live empty lives. This is a glorious old world, but our privilege of living in it necessarily brings certain obligations to us.

I have always felt that I owe an everlasting obligation to others who in the early days helped me blaze the trail and lay the foundation of my life. It is an obligation which cannot be paid in dollars and cents.

Certainly we all have obligations which can be met only by the faithful discharge of our duties.

Obstacles Mean Strength

DEMOSTHENES, THE GREATEST of all orators, as a boy had an impediment of speech which he conquered by placing pebbles in his mouth and shouting. Beethoven, one of the world's greatest composers, was deaf. Milton, the great poet, was blind. The pages of history record accounts of men who have succeeded in spite of obstacles. With some of them the handicaps were poverty, ill health and poor education; others were maimed physically, but even this did not stop them.

It is a natural thing to want to succeed, but all are not willing to pay the price of success. Some folks have a wishbone instead of a backbone. They are not willing to subject themselves to hard labor in order to plant the seeds of their ambition. They want to reap benefits, but without much work. They can see easily how the law of cause and effect must work for others, but they expect to have it suspended in their own case. Too many people believe in pull when they should be thinking about push. There is really no excuse for failure; there never have been such splendid opportunities on every hand. There is a dearth of men capable of handling big things. It takes hard work and years of study to fit one's self for the larger responsibilities of life.

Cultivate vision and foresight by having confidence in yourself and in others, and by having faith in an all-wise, benevolent, overruling Power.

Who Is Greatest?

THAT WOMAN teaching in yonder school house at the crossroads is frequently a larger asset to the community than many a well-to-do taxpayer who doles out her salary with painful regret.

That preacher, dependent upon the generosity of the congregation to which he ministers, is worth more to the neighborhood in which he lives, in dollars and cents, in inspiration to its children and youth, than Mr. Highbrow up there on the hill who lives for the filling of his own barns and the pleasures of his family.

What, then, is the intrinsic value of an individual in the community? The emphasis has been unwisely placed by some on wealth and power. Men are not great or small because of their material possessions. They are great or small because of *what they are*.

world. . . . They are not of the world, even as I am not of the world. . . . As thou hast sent me into the world, even so have I also sent them into the world" (John 17:15–18). Plainly, then, the Christian is designed to live in this world, work in it, laugh and weep in it, succeed and fail in it, but is not to be worldly, i.e., like those who are not Christian.

The Use Of Today

WHAT WE ARE tomorrow and the next day and the day after that depends upon our use of today. The tools that our hands now grasp will carve our future and govern our activities in times ahead. Comparatively few people accept seriously the advice of others in vital matters until their own experience, however bitter, may have confirmed the words of their friends.

Just the same, out of my own experience and observation I am once again passing the good word along. We owe that much to those who come after us as well as to those who travel with us.

Why Should A Man Give?

IT HAS BEEN said that human nature is extremely selfish and that if one makes a sacrifice, he does so expecting something in return. I do not share in this belief. There are many thoroughly unselfish people in this world. My mother was unselfish and no doubt you can say the same of your mother. Mothers go down into the valley of the shadow to bring to this world their most precious treasures, with the hope that they will become worth-while men and women.

My life and yours have not been given us to while away. As stewards, we must render the greatest worth-while service. Therefore, sooner or later, there must come a day of accounting. If we have lived for self alone, the figures will be in the red. If we have been thoroughly unselfish, and have given for the advancement of others, the balance will be on the right side.

We should give because giving develops a generous nature, and we become a channel through which God ministers to the benefit of the needy and worthy.

Living The Christian Life

IT IS PLAIN fact that *if you and I are to live a Christian life at all it will be in our world as it is now—today!* Perhaps we have prayed "Thy kingdom come, Thy will be done on earth as it is in heaven," so often that subconsciously we feel something miraculous is going to occur without our doing much about it, and that we will awaken some fine morning to find that kingdom benevolently enfolding us. Not so, my friends, not so! We will have to do a great deal about it, for if we live the good life of faith, it will be in the environment wherein "we live and move" and have our everyday being. The farmer must live it upon the farm, the merchant in the store, the mechanic in the shop, and the banker in the bank. Every man's life, no matter where or how it may be lived, presents both the opportunity and the demand for forthright, consistent Christian living.

It will not do to say, "My environment, the people with whom I am compelled to associate, the place where I work, make it impossible for me to be the kind of Christian I would like to be." Jesus gives to all who will seek it the power either to rise superior to environment, or to move out into a better one. Remember, the apostle Paul said there were "saints" in Nero's very household.

Just before leaving the upper room for the Garden of Gethsemane Jesus prayed for His disciples. This is what He said: "I pray not that thou shouldst take them out of the

Bitter Competition

THE WORLD IN which we live is big enough for each of us to express his largest capacities without personal injury to another. No one need ever feel the bitterness which competition sometimes provokes unnecessarily. The world has a place for the largest service we are capable of rendering, and service never need be an infringement upon another's rights.

Life offers opportunities as large as we are capable of filling. There should never be unfriendly rivalry. If the place occupied by us is not large enough to accomplish our best results, then let us make our present position a larger and a more important one.

The surest road to promotion is ability to promote. They who enter upon their tasks possessed of the spirit of bitter rivalry, of inordinate ambition and selfish greed, can never hope to reach the desired goal.

Happiness Versus Pleasure

SUPREME HAPPINESS of life cannot be found in any one thing we have or can gain. Whence the source of happiness? Happiness and pleasure must not be confused, for they are not the same. One rests upon lasting foundations, while the other is generally found in passing incidents and experiences in our daily activities.

Happiness results from spiritual ideals at least partially realized. It does not depend upon material things or outward circumstances. Indeed, the things and circumstances generally regarded as requirements for happiness actually play a very small part in the experience of this much-to-be-desired condition.

A large number of people are seeking happiness in the wrong place, by the wrong methods. There is only one way to find happiness, and that is in the pathway of service. Money acquired and position attained can never result in happiness, except as they are used to benefit the condition of those outside our household.

The broader obligation is placed upon us—that of ministering unto others—and in this duty, happily accepted, is found the necessary experience which permits the spiritual idealism to find its own happiest environment.

Pity the man who is looking for happiness in accumulating houses, automobiles, increased store holdings, social opportunities and such things as may be acquired. Happiness is not found in them. Happiness is native only to the soul seeking to serve others, that they may have a share in the larger and better things of life.

Happiness is not without, but like the Kingdom of Heaven, it is within those who serve.

Reliability

RELIABILITY IS AT the very heart of business. The business world is bound together and firmly held by that brand of cement known as reliability.

A man's word must prove as good as his bond, or he fails to place his business before the public in the most favorable manner. Business failures are not the result so much of the business *per se* as from the men undertaking to carry it on, and failure to put into the business the necessary requirements to make it succeed.

The Larger Task

ALMOST EVERY young man looks forward to the day when he will have placed upon him a larger opportunity and responsibility. That attitude is both normal and commendable. The know-how to possess that desired experience is the one problem.

"I wish I knew how to secure a better position than the one I have," declared an ambitious young man. There is an answer to that "wish" and it is this: Prove your ability to manage the desired position and when the opportunity comes for you to be advanced, you will be ready.

The larger task is just ahead of every man. Some will advance while others will remain at a standstill. However, all motion does not mean progress. A small boy will enjoy his rocking horse for hours; he will have an abundance of motion, but will make no progress. Just so with some people if they are busy as can be with a lot of little things that get them nowhere. Not mere motion, but progress—going ahead with something—is the requirement in the attainment of the larger task.

He Leads Who Follows

IT IS A self-evident truth that a man who is to become a good leader must first learn to follow, or in other words, to obey orders. His very first lesson is to learn to obey himself.

A man must so regulate his habits that he can rise at a certain hour, be temperate in all things, and refrain from undesirable language, gossiping, fault-finding and from unjustly criticizing others. He must control his temper, prevent himself from worrying about matters over which he has no power, and adopt systematic routines of study as well as of recreation. He must deal fairly and honestly, show increasing interest in his work, be economical, industrious, cheerful, patient and persevering. He must possess initiative, have good health and be courageous in all his dealings.

"The man who controls himself is greater than the general who controls an army." There is an abundance of truth in this statement.

Thrift

THRIFT MEANS nothing more than living within your income. You cannot hope to succeed in a business way unless you grasp the real meaning of thrift. The world's greatest financiers are self-made men who learned early in life the absolute necessity of keeping their expenditures within their income.

Thrift does not mean hoarding. It means efficiency; making the most of your opportunity; a saving of time; elimination of lost motion.

Thrift is economic preparedness. It conserves, increases and distributes the wealth, develops and trains the mind, ennobles and strengthens the character.

Thrift teaches good management by imposing system, regularity and promptness. By practice these virtues soon become habits.

Thrift develops our sense of values. We learn that little wastes are big wastes in the aggregate. We learn that we must be patient; that though at times our savings may seem to increase with discouraging slowness there is compensation on ahead.

Thrift gives foresight. It causes us to subordinate present inviting plans to some larger future purpose. It leads to economic independence and therefore adds to our self-respect. It represents mental as well as economic soundness.

Thrift makes possible participation in the worth-while activities of our communities. Thrift teaches us self-denial and persistence. It strengthens our will and steadies our purpose by giving us a fixed goal.

Thrift conserves and uses rightly our time, and our material, physical, mental and moral resources.

Look Around You

THE MAN OF great power finds great opportunity. And the man of small power similarly finds only small opportunity. But the opportunity is never a thousand miles away. Big or small, it is always close at hand; often it is just a trifle beyond a man's reach.

We think a lot about success afar off, for it is human nature to imagine ourselves working in the wrong place. But the fact is that right here where our simplest job is waiting for us, we shall find our Great Expectations, for success loves to hide behind—what? Why, behind the simplest job!

Modern Proverbs

MANY MEN ARE endowed by nature with a pleasing personality. People want to go to them and to deal with them. If a man is not born with his smiling, exhilarating personality, it is possible to cultivate it.

*   *   *

Almost any dream can come true, provided there is truth in the vision and provided you sincerely give yourself to the dream's development.

*   *   *

Do not pass judgment upon your fellow men and their work until you have seen and heard the evidence.

*   *   *

A young man of ordinary mind and body, with ordinary talents, led on by a great ambition, will accomplish far more than the man of the finest mental and physical equipment who drifts.

*   *   *

No serious man should have time for the mediocre in any phase of his living.

The Timeless "Now"

IT IS DIFFICULT for us not to live in the past as we grow older. It is just as difficult for us not to live in the future. But it is when we improve and enjoy the timeless *now* that we justify the past and prepare for the future. Vain regrets assail us when we neglect to accept opportunities to better our condition. Equally vain regrets come to us when we fail to extend a helping hand or to speak an encouraging word to another struggling on life's way. How easy it is to plan good that we shall do tomorrow while we lose sight of blessings which we may now share.

Yesterday, with its neglect of opportunities, is gone forever. But tomorrow is always within reach. Striving to live in any time but the present is futile and demoralizing.

Responsibility

RESPONSIBILITY IS ALWAYS a sign of trust. As business develops, the young man's life is not made easier, but as responsibilities become greater, he has the greater strength to bear them.

I know of a man who at one time realized his inability to cope with the many vexatious problems which confronted him daily. Seated at his desk, he said to himself, "I am going to master this business so that if anyone in this establishment wants to know anything about it, he must come to me."

And he did it! Today he is an unusual man in his field, but it took more than dreaming and thinking for this to happen.

Any young man who takes as much interest in the business of his employer as he would in his own, is bound to succeed. One should always work with this in mind: "I intend to make myself so indispensable to this business that my firm cannot get along without me."

Thus business develops a man. It makes him think until thinking is a habit. If he thinks and acts constructively, providing his mode of conduct is right, he is well nigh certain to be a success.

Study

THERE MAY BE those who say they have lost, if they ever had it, the faculty for study. They tell us they find no fascination in books. We grant such a deplorable condition possible, but what then? Why not cultivate a taste for study? Why not seek to re-acquire a fondness for those things which study alone assures? Why not try to learn how to appreciate the joys that result from mental effort? The time spent in the pursuit of knowledge and understanding is rewarded by a realization of ideals and a growth in power and determination.

Books readily or easily understood are seldom worth the time consumed in reading them. Cultivate a taste for the Good, the Better, the Best—the most profitable study. "The finest reading is in the Book of Books."

Don't Be An Automaton

DETERMINE TO DO some thinking for yourself. Don't live entirely upon the thoughts of others. Plan to use the brain God has given you as carefully as possible. Study to use your own head and hands, and to control your own heart.

Boys learn to swim by trying within the safety zone. They expend effort, and they even realize that they are taking some risk. Thus do men learn to take the initiative. They practice within reach of safety, and as their ability increases, they move out a little farther into the deeper possibilities of life.

No one is expected to succeed one hundred per cent in the use of his judgment. Seeming failure sometimes results in spite of our best judgment. Normal conditions sometimes change, and the best result that can possibly come to the man seeking to direct his affairs is to teach him the new channel in which to direct his mental activities.

Seek first of all to think of yourself relative to some of the smaller problems and less perplexing situations. Put the calmer deliberations of your mind in matters where the involvements are not too great nor too serious. Study to discover how others have become thinkers, planners and executors of splendid undertakings. Summon the best you have and all you can command to the accomplishment of the task considered, and remember that God meant you for victory and not defeat. To have dominion is your mission.

Therefore, work, read, think, meditate, commune with the Source of Wisdom, seeking Him to guide your undertakings.

Don't be an automaton.

Business Finances

THE TROUBLE WITH the average small-town merchant is that he gets his pockets mixed. Instead of living on the money in his own pocket, he often lives on that in the pocket of his business. He does not run his business as a thing distinct in itself. He confuses himself with it and so begins to think that he and the business are one; that its profits are his to use as he will; that its current cash is always available for his passing needs and pleasures. The financial well-being of his business, however small, must remain intact in order that it may thrive on its own increase.

Cooperation In Life

THERE IS NOTHING that will develop a man more than to make him responsible for certain results. It takes a big man to believe in other men, to entrust his affairs to them, and having done so, to discharge anxiety from the mind. It is the narrow-minded man who thinks that no one can do a thing quite as well as he, himself, and who refuses to delegate any authority or responsibility to other people. Such a man cannot hope to succeed, for he is unable to cooperate in the fullest sense.

Cooperation often means sacrifice. It became necessary for both North and South to make tremendous sacrifices to maintain the integrity of the Union. It took a bloody war and a great loss of life to teach us the lesson. But out of that disaster was born a new nation, each state now cooperating to make our country the strongest nation on earth.

The human body is one of the best examples of cooperation. Nature has her way of telling us when any organ is not doing its full duty. And how happy we are when, in full health, every organ in the body is cooperating and functioning as it should. The result is that we can accomplish more, and our labors become a pleasure instead of a drudgery.

Memorial Day

WHAT DOES Memorial Day mean to us? Just another vacation with a visit to the cemetery, where we place flowers upon the graves of those we have loved and lost awhile?

It should mean infinitely more than this. It should mean a time of personal dedication to the ideals for which others gave their lives and to the institutions of our national and religious life, for which others went to death.

It should mean for us the stirring of memory and the upward look. This day should place upon our lips the testimony of gratitude for all that the brave and unselfish have done to bring the world a little nearer God's ideal for man. It should leave within our hearts a high resolve to go forward doing our best to help complete the unfinished tasks.

The Rounded Man

THE MAN WHO is the greatest good to any organization is the full-rounded man who is developed physically and mentally. There is one other very important factor, the most important, for it has to do with eternity—our spiritual development. What are we fitting ourselves to do when we have shuffled off this mortal coil? Business and money and worldly goods are all right as far as they go, but no greater mistake can be made than to put in all our time acquiring wealth, and leaving nothing but riches on this side when we enter the Great Beyond.

A little thought along this line will make a man more unselfish and mindful of the interests of others. With jealousy and selfishness eliminated, the individual becomes a better citizen.

The man who really does things, needs no monument to perpetuate his memory. His influence lives long after he is gone.

The well-rounded person has three distinct powers—physical, mental, and spiritual. The development of any one at the expense of the others will cause a man to be one-sided, whereas through the development of all three, the man becomes a truly rounded individual. This is the kind of man who will keep an organization strong and virile.

The Difference

IT IS EASY to copy someone else. By the same token it takes courage and fortitude to be different. The ways in which you are just like other men never get you anywhere. You must make your way on the difference. It is your cornerstone. You can build on nothing else.

Your difference sets you off from other men. Some men have even made an asset of a difference which could have been a defeat or a limitation. Robert Louis Stevenson suffered all his life and often did his writing propped up in bed. Joseph Pulitzer was blind for many years, but he worked and developed his great property. Theodore Roosevelt was a puny child; he turned himself into a veritable giant.

In your makeup—physical, mental or moral—somewhere in that which is called your personality, there is an element of ability, of genius, of absolute greatness. The thing for you to do is to find and develop it.

Criticism

BLESSED BE CRITICISM! It always should be welcome for the real good it does. It should be thoughtfully received and considered because of the kindly motivation with which it is given.

Intelligent criticism is never crude or rude. It is neither unkind nor unjust. It bespeaks a personal interest and solicitude. A real critic need not be feared, for he is a friend. Why is it then that so many are fearful of the critic? Because a vast majority of "critics" are not critics at all. One of the easiest mistakes one can make is to conclude that he is a critic when actually he is only finding fault or giving an expression of personal opinion colored by prejudice.

To find fault does not require any special degree of intelligence or information. Real criticism is an expression of a cooperative attitude of mind. Its purpose is to build up and to establish. A mere fault-finding disposition never constructs, but tears down, discourages and atrophies human effort. Bring on your criticism, but be sure it *is* criticism.

What about finding fault? Stop it. If you have never done it, don't begin it. What about expressing one's opinion? It is entirely proper to do so if one keeps in mind that personal opinion should always be given and received solely as personal opinion. It may be valid, or it may not be valid.

Criticism intelligently and kindly placed will always spur an honest man to greater activities and more heroic effort to reach the higher goals of life. There is a story that Plato was told that boys in the street were laughing at his singing. His reply was, "Then I must learn to sing better."

Prosperity

THE DICTIONARY DEFINES prosperity as "the attainment of the object desired." Is it something we get, and then sit back and enjoy? Does it mean a Utopia when we have enough money to quit work and take in the sights? Or is it the opportunity to live our lives, be active in body, spirit and mind, in such a way that the finer things arouse in us appreciation and happiness?

Attainment of one objective should be but a momentary resting place in preparation for further effort which will bring a greater degree of happiness. Life is a process of continual growth. Therein lies prosperity and happiness.

Cooperation

ONE MAN CAN do only so much, but when he identifies others with himself for the accomplishment of a certain purpose, not only does his own work become easier, but the results more certain.

If a man will arrange his time and plan a definite schedule for his daily work, he will find that each hour will cooperate with the others, thereby creating a system, or in other words, a track, for him to run on. You have, no doubt, noticed that a busy man always has time to spare, and the reason is, he has his work so planned that he can execute it with dispatch. The man who is always crowded for time is, as a general rule, the man who has not his daily routine properly organized.

We must all cooperate with one another. By so doing, we are in tune with our duties and with God.

Directing Your Life

YOU ARE HERE with a life to use, invest, and develop. Where would you rather use it? How would you prefer to invest it? Through what channel would you choose to develop it? Taking into account your personal ability and the amount of effort you are willing to give to its enlargement, what would you rather do and become than any other one thing?

Your answer will mean your success in life. It may not mean you will accumulate material riches, but you will morally develop your deeper self in the interest of the larger life. It will mean that you will come into possession of those riches of the soul which can never be taken from you. You will have a lasting pride in the thing you are doing.

The Story Of The Talents

YOU REMEMBER THE parable in the Bible regarding the talents. To one man God gave five talents; to another, two; to another, one. The one who received five talents went and traded with them and gained five additional talents. Likewise, the one who received two gained another two. But he who received one, digged in the earth and hid his Lord's money away. To the first the Lord said, "Well done, thou good and faithful servant. Thou hast been faithful over a few things, I will make you ruler over many things." So likewise He said to the one to whom He had given two talents. But to him who buried his talent, the Lord said, "Thou wicked and slothful servant, go and give thy one talent to him who hath ten talents."

To him and to his kind the Lord's words are still directed with all the force of old: "Cast ye the unprofitable servant out into outer darkness." So the man who makes use of his talents is blessed abundantly, and the one who fails to employ his gifts profitably is usually the one who makes excuses for his failure in life, saying he never had an opportunity.

Industry is mechanical action following upon creative thought, the character of which is reflected by the individual. If his thoughts are constructive, his labor is bound to produce results. It is a pleasure when one determines to do the task better than it has ever been done before, for when we engage in our duties with vim and determination to succeed, our work becomes play. Thus we find pleasure in self-expression.

He who has discovered this joy has discovered the secret of happiness. Thus do we see the wonderful justice in the Biblical injunction, "As you sow so shall you also reap."

He Did Pretty Well!

MY OWN EXPERIENCE teaches me that if one is sufficiently thirsty for knowledge, an elaborate school building and all the gadgets that go with it, highly desirable though they may be, are not absolutely essential. The little one-room schoolhouse, made of logs in the days of the pioneers, and a few books, have formed the educational foundation of many of the greatest men of the ages. Even the absence of these simple, rudimentary advantages need not constitute a barrier to knowledge. You are every one familiar with the story of a young man in Illinois, who, having no money, borrowed books and learned mathematics by working out problems upon the back of a wooden fire shovel with a bit of charcoal by the light of a fireplace. That young man grew up, became a lawyer, was elected President of the United States and wrote the immortal Gettysburg Address. Abraham Lincoln did pretty well!

Who Serves Best?

The Great Teacher declared, "And whosoever will be chief among you, let him be your servant."

He serves best who gives most of himself. Self is forgotten by the one who serves, for such a one rejoices to see success coming to others through his efforts.

He serves best who forgets time. There are no rigid hours of work for the true servant. Whether one realizes it or not, there is no time when the good servant is not developing his power of service.

He serves best who makes the best use of his talents. Repeated study of how to serve best brings about greater capacity for service and the development of every talent.

He serves best who is faithful, loyal, industrious, alert and who seeks opportunities to use every talent in the interest of others. The best service will bring rewards of happiness, contentment and joy. Tasks become a pleasure and life is larger and fuller.

Pity Him And Help Him

MEN AND WOMEN grow old and fall by the wayside of life feeling that they have been failures largely because they have been trying to accomplish some tasks for which they were never fitted—in which they had no real personal delight and to which they could not bring an ever-springing fountain of enthusiasm. This does not mean that they were necessarily engaged in unimportant, unprofitable, or even unmoral work. It does mean, however, that they were in the wrong places where their personal usefulness never could be realized.

Pity the one who has fallen into the wrong place, who never takes pride in his work, whose enthusiasm never reaches white heat, and whose sole interest is merely that of bread and butter. Pity him and help him.

Men Of Vision

A MAN BECOMES a visionary when he sees and plans, but fails to act; or when he plans without a purpose. Vision implies that which is creative, perceiving, planning, building, developing, progressing and attaining. It is evident that no man can succeed who has not a vision, for he is mentally blind and sees no further than the present. Neither is it possible for him to succeed unless he is determined to pursue his purpose steadfastly.

It is said that as far as the range of mental vision is concerned, there are four classes of human beings. First, the mentally blind, who see no further than the present; second, the general who plans for a year; third, the genius who plans for a lifetime; fourth, the seer and prophet who plans for generations yet to be.

The man mentally blind is actuated by his own selfish motives, living unto himself, with little thought for his fellowman. He is the man who, after he has acquired a competency, retires early in life to enjoy what he has accumulated. But the man of vision and purpose has no such intention. He is interested in something more than the acquisition of material things. He is interested in the welfare of society and in humanity in general. He endeavors to lead a life-long existence of usefulness and influence.

What a vision our forefathers had, to formulate a government by and for the people, a government that has stood the test for many decades and today causes our nation to be regarded as the leader in world activities!

Giving Themselves

SOME MEN ATTAIN positions of distinction in the business world and are entrusted with responsibilities involving the well-being of hundreds of their fellows, while others never get beyond the village store or the country office. But again and again I find that those who are in positions too generally regarded as insignificant are doing so much for their communities and for the people with whom they associate, that others in spectacular positions would be shamed by comparison.

Why is this? Because these unknown people are giving everything they have to their tasks and unselfishly counting their gains by service returns.

The Golden Rule

No MAN, in my opinion, can pull himself up by his own boot-straps. He is hoisted by his personal efforts and the cooperative efforts of his friends. There are few martyrs to success; chiefly they exist in the bilious imaginations of the envious and embittered failures.

In business, true, there is a survival of the fittest, but the fittest is synonymous with the one who practices most consistently the cardinal virtues of being patient, humble, diligent, charitable and honest.

To my idea, the one rule to which an ambitious young man or woman can adhere and remain morally safe, is the Golden Rule. In it are encompassed all commandments and conventions; though it and it only can success and happiness be derived.

II
IN OUR DAILY TASKS

Why Do Men Work?

IT IS NOT enough to say that men work to get a living, or to raise a family, or to pay the bills. A great many men with vastly more money than they could ever need for these purposes have nevertheless worked harder than the majority of mankind.

There must be something in the impulse to work that has nothing to do with the butcher's bill. We cannot explain the impulse that we have pointed out on the assumption that men work for the sake of living day by day. Can we say, then, that true men work to find a congenial and useful form of self-expression and self-betterment?

There is in us something that craves work, something that wants and demands it, and in a good many of us something that loves it. We feel that an activity which allows us to labor at something worth-while satisfies a fundamental element of nature.

But we make still another demand on work. It must make us better in soul, mind and body.

Organization

THE FIVE SEPARATE fingers are five independent units. Close them and the fist multiplies strength. This is organization. The thought forcefully reminds me of a story.

A man had seven sons who continually found fault with one another. This worried the father. One day he called them together and handing them a bundle of sticks, requested that it be broken. Each man strained every nerve and finally handed the bundle back, saying, "It cannot be done." The father cut the string and broke each stick separately, and the sons exclaimed, "Easy enough to do it so." The incident served his purpose and demonstrated to the sons that "in union there is strength." Each man for himself can do little in the world, but by cooperating with others he can become a power.

On every hand we observe where the unified efforts of many men have a tremendous advantage over the efforts of a single individual. A successful organization is a group of capable men of character and ability pursuing a worthy cause. Their efforts, directed with intelligence and energy, produce the highest average of results to the unit they represent. Therefore, the success of an organization depends upon the character of the men who comprise it. One might as well try to equip an army with imbeciles, cripples, and an occasional vigorous man; or attempt to build a house with rotten timber, as to run an organization well with men who lack character.

It is very important that the organization executives be men of vision and purposes. They must be keenly alive to the possibilities of securing the cooperation of their associates.

Honesty In Business

THE INFLUENCE of a business leader's example reaches much further than his own activities. It is becoming the rule rather than the exception to deal justly and refuse to perform the petty chicanery which was formerly considered a permissible part of business procedure. We are proving that it is good business to label merchandise accurately, to give thirty-six inches to every yard, and to deliver sixteen ounces to the pound.

Far-seeing business leaders govern their lives and transactions in accordance with their religious beliefs. Anyone who is honestly skeptical on this point can find proof that wealth may be amassed more easily through honest than through dishonest methods, and that square dealing reduces the mental and physical strain to a minimum.

The single source of lasting satisfaction to the businessman, then, is the knowledge that he has rendered an honest service in exchange for every dollar received.

The Golden Rule In Business

I STARTED my first retail store back in 1902, in a small coal-mining town in southwestern Wyoming. Once it was established, I needed men—and I needed men whom I could trust to build careers themselves in the business. I chose them carefully, it is true, but I can tell you now that my confidence in those men provided the incentive for their personal and business growth. That confidence, that faith in men and their basic impulses to do the right thing, helped to build a business which now embraces 1,650 retail stores, with a yearly volume of over a billion dollars.

That first little store I called "The Golden Rule." Shrewd merchants and bankers laughed at me and the principles I had solemnly laid down for myself and my business. "He'll learn," they said. "He'll soon find out that it doesn't pay to trust people, and to try to drag religious ideas into business."

But these prophets of doom were wrong. I found that the Golden Rule is a practical rule for business as it is for the business of living. If a man is willing to do unto others as he expects them to do unto him, he will find that, far from giving more than he gets, he will get more than he gives. That has been my experience.

Good merchandise and fair prices began to win the confidence of my customers, and my first store grew into two, then four, and so on. Therefore I can tell you that the Golden Rule is actually a rule of enlightened SELF-interest.

Cooperation In Mechanics

THINK OF THE intricate mechanism of a watch with its escapement and balance wheels, its pivots, jewels, and numerous little screws. The slightest variation will throw the whole assemblage of parts out of order. With what precision the different parts must work, in order that the watch may become a satisfactory timepiece!

Then there is the automobile. How it acts when the spark plugs become dirty, or the carburetor becomes choked, or when the gas is below standard! But when every part is in working order, the motor represents power, which, if rightly controlled, becomes a servant to do one's bidding.

So it is in business. No one man connected with a company who has achieved a phenomenal success could go out into the business world and accomplish alone what he has done with his organization; for not only has he had the opportunity to use his own knowledge, but that of dozens and hundreds of his associates.

Competition Is Good Business

YOU HAVE NO better friend in business than your best competitor. Fifty years as a merchant has taught me that again and again.

One day some years ago, to give you an example, we received a frantic telegram from one of our store managers. A mail-order chain, he reported, was negotiating for space right beside our store in his western town. "Please," he wired, "do everything you can to keep them from getting it."

It happened that the landlord from whom we leased our space there also owned the vacant store. Our manager hoped that, through this connection, we would be able to block the entrance of this competitor.

Rest assured we gave our manager a quick reply, but this was the gist of it: "On the contrary, we shall do everything to assist the competitor in getting his lease. You will find him an excellent neighbor and a good competitor. He will bring more business into the area—and you'll get your share, never fear."

It worked out just that way. Customers came into the new store out of curiosity, they shopped, and then went into the older stores and shopped some more. The net result was *more* business for everyone.

That story exposes the fallacy underlying fears of competition—the mistaken belief that there is only a limited amount of business in any given area, and that additional stores mean that each one's share must be cut that much thinner. It simply is not true. If a man does a good job, his competitor needn't worry him. A merchant who approaches business with the idea of serving the public well has nothing to fear from competition, however much of it there may be. In business, as elsewhere, we are our own pacemakers.

The Emerson Story

Mr. Harrington Emerson entered the office of President Ripley of the Santa Fe Railroad and said, "I can save your road a million dollars a year."

"How can you do it?" inquired the railroad president.

"That is my secret. You give me the opportunity and pay me if I do; and if I do not, then do not pay me," replied the efficiency expert.

Mr. Emerson was employed and at once had posters hung all over the system that read, "Get the Safety Habit." Everybody soon began to think and talk safety, and at the end of the first year, more than a million dollars had been saved in wrecks prevented and accident fees avoided.

The further result—and the greater one—is that today every railroad has Safety First Committees. The idea has become interwoven into the very fabric of our entire system of rail traffic.

We can all profit by this lesson.

84   L<small>INES OF A</small> L<small>AYMAN</small>

scores of examples of manufacturers, wholesalers and retailers who voluntarily put the Golden Rule to work in their relations with employees, competitors and customers.

The Capable Salesman

A GOOD SALESMAN possesses initiative; he does not wait until he is told to do a thing. He is observant, careful, and diligent. He has the same interest in the business as if it were his own. He is industrious, for when he is not employed in selling, he is arranging his stock so as to wait on trade with the least possible delay.

Once, when I was a boy and in my first position, I had a customer for an overcoat. It was the policy of the store to turn customers over to other salesmen, rather than have them go out unsold. I had tried, I thought, every line of argument. The customer had said, "Well, I will look around and see if I can do any better."

I began to be nervous, for I did not want to miss the sale. I went to the proprietor and told him that I could not sell the customer, and everyone else was busy. He looked squarely at me, spoke rather sharply, and said, "Sell him yourself!"

I went back and sold the overcoat. Thus, I had learned my first lesson in perseverance. It does not pay to give up too quickly. He can who thinks he can.

Making A Merchant

I HAVE OFTEN observed ambitious young men and women going to night school to acquire a better education. That kind of determination is not found in ordinary people. They are the kind of people who are ready to open the door when Opportunity comes to knock.

We have started a number of young men in our stores on a nominal salary, in some cases a mere living. Our object was to encourage in them the practice of economy. It has been our idea to help these young men for the future. We have insisted on a careful training. Each young man must sweep, open boxes, wash windows and do stock work. These duties are humble but important ones. A store should be kept as clean and tidy as a proud housewife keeps her home.

To be a good stock-keeper is one of the important attainments of a merchant. Not only does this apply to keeping stock clean, but free from odds and ends. Take for instance, a dozen shirts: One must sell ten of them in order to pay the manufacturer. The two that are left represent the merchant's profit, and he has made no money on the dozen shirts until he has sold these two.

The young man's knowledge of business will depend largely upon his ability to grasp fundamental principles. He should be taught first the value of truthful statements; to make good every statement; to be courteous and pleasant in all his dealings.

If a young man will submit himself to this program in the

same spirit that a man submits himself to college demands, the training he will get will be worth thousands of dollars to him.

Good Judgment Applied

IN ORDER TO succeed in business, a man must possess sound judgment based on knowledge and experience. He must know values. He must be a good judge of how and when to buy, and, above all, he must know how much to buy. Many men are ruined by getting so deeply in debt they can never get out. They allow their ambition to get the better of their judgment. They forget to protect themselves against the uncertainties of business life. Hence, in time of stress they are crowded by their creditors who demand their money.

Besides being a judge of values, a man should be a judge of human nature. Dealing with the public offers one of the greatest opportunities for education there is. Every customer is different. Each one demands personal attention along the lines of his preferences and individual viewpoint.

Taking Stock

THE IMPORTANT THING to do after taking stock of ourselves at the end of the calendar year is to charge off for depreciation, just as a good merchant will make allowance for merchandise that may have become out of date. Thus, if we overestimate our worth, we are liable to discover an error in our inventory, which always leads to disappointment.

Be fair with yourself, and take your loss on the start resolving that from now on you are going to get results for every effort expended. By this I do not mean monetary results, but rather the results that cause a man to become bigger, broader and better. Look up and press forward. Be tolerant of the wishes of others. Be charitable in your view. Be open and honest in all your thoughts and actions.

It is always the start that requires the greatest effort. We are prone to live on as we did yesterday and become too easily satisfied with our results. In my business career I have often heard it said, "The world owes me a living. I have only one life to live and I am going to have a good time." What a grievous mistake such folks are making. There is only one result for them and it is inevitable. In the evening of life, when they are unable to work as they once did, they will find themselves with too little in the storehouse to provide for their requirements.

Seeking Correction

ONE DAY EARLY in my business life I went to my employer and said, "Tell me about my faults in order that I may correct them."

Quick as a flash he replied, "If I should do that, you might, in your effort to correct them, overlook some of your good qualities. Keep on plugging, doing the best you know how each day of your life, and eventually you will come out victorious."

I realized, then, that I wanted to grow too fast. I was not content to plant the seed and wait for the harvest. I wanted to sow and reap at the same time. I soon realized that this was not only wrong, but impossible. I found that if I was to build a durable foundation, it would take time. So, regardless of all my anxiety and discouragements, I stayed. I was learning a fact which I have seen most admirably expressed by Mr. Edmond Guggenheim:

"Choose a career which appeals to you most and avoid the danger of being diverted from that career by the possibility of immediately earning what would seem at the time to be a large salary."

Success Does Not Need Genius

THE DISTINGUISHED English author, the late H. G. Wells, said:
"Success has absolutely nothing whatever to do with a
man's reputation, or material possessions, or social
prominence.

"True success is the relation between what a man is today
(that is what he has finally become) and what he could have
become had he made the most of his ability and opportunity
through all the years of his working life."

It is an astonishing contrast that Mr. Wells makes in the
two conditions: (1) not what anyone of us is in the later years
of life, but (2) what we *could* have become had we done the
utmost with all our ability, understanding, and control
directed upon a worth-while ultimate purpose.

This means that a young man starting out can so increase
and direct his effort that it will carry him far beyond the
usual time of men's retirement. Let me say this of retirement:
No man should live a business life of 20 or 30 years and then
retire into *nothing*. Along the way he should have provided
for himself *something* into which to retire; something worth-
while as an adventure in benefits and service.

Success in business does not depend upon genius. Any
young man of ordinary intelligence who is morally sound and
not afraid to work should succeed in spite of obstacles and
handicaps if he plays the game fairly and keeps everlastingly
at it. When I see a youngster identifying himself so closely
with his work that the closing hour passes unheeded, I recognize the beginnings of success. He is doing more than is re-

quired of him—that is, he is doing more than his employer requires of him, but not more than his own conscience requires.

Human Nature

A STUDY OF human nature develops tact. It is not so much what one says as how one says it. No man can be a success as a businessman who has not the power of self-control. The patience of a salesman is often tried to the utmost, but the trained man will not show it. He takes the same pains with the lady who desires to match a piece of lace as he does with a man who wants a suit of clothes. There may be little money in the sale of the lace, but the woman wants it perhaps as much as the man wants the suit. If the customer is slighted because her wants are small, she is likely to go elsewhere when she makes a larger purchase.

I remember well, that when I was a salesman myself, I made it a point to wait on those customers other clerks considered hard to suit. Many of them later became splendid customers, for it is human nature to appreciate any special courtesy.

I Changed My Mind

ONE MORNING a large man wearing a great sombrero entered
the store in the West where I clerked. He intended to start a
store in another community. He said that he had been watching me for some time and that he felt I could manage his new
enterprise. He offered me practically twice as much as I was
then receiving.

I was very much impressed with the proposition. My wife
favored it too, and so when Mr. Johnson, my employer, returned, I told him I was contemplating a change. He looked
at me searchingly and said, "Why, I thought you were happy
here." He talked with me for a little while and though he
made me no promises, he caused me to feel that, after all, the
larger salary in immediate prospect was not everything.

I recalled my decision, stayed with Mr. Johnson and I
know now that I made no mistake. Friends have said that
things would have happened just as they have, even if I had
accepted what looked like a larger opportunity. I feel dif-
ferently about it. It was not a larger salary that I needed then;
it was experience with the right kind of people. Though I did
not realize it, I was laying a foundation. The man under
whose guidance I worked was interested not only in the foundation, he was interested in me. I have never forgotten him.

The Years Ahead

THE YEARS AHEAD will bring new merchandising into our business enterprises. New standards will be developed. In countless ways changes will be everywhere in evidence. But the fundamental principles of business will prevail. Honesty will reign above cleverness and chicanery. Industry will outstrip spasmodic and inconsistent brilliance.

The men who succeed will continue to be those who work hard, without watching the clock. Of even greater importance, they will plan while they work! Men must think straight in order to get the best results from long hours of hard work. They must continue to cleave to the foundation principles of their enterprises.

Honor bespeaks worth.

Confidence begets trust.

Service brings satisfaction.

Cooperation proves the quality of leadership.

Responsibility For Others

WE HAVE MADE great progress in business practices. If we are to consolidate past gains and advance, we in business must give time and effort, which are not always immediately productive of profits, to the training of our successors. We have this responsibility to the vocation which gives us our livelihood—but we should be glad to do it for the sake of the young men themselves. I sincerely believe that we who employ should build something into a man instead of constantly taking something out of him. So I shall offer this advice:

Do not primarily train men to work. Train them to serve willingly and intelligently.

Do not train men merely to obey orders that they may or may not fully understand. Train them to study the job, to develop perception of what is to be done, then to turn loose upon it fully their understanding, initiative, and effort.

Do not train men merely to be your shadow. Train them to bring as much of their ability into action as they can reach, deep down in themselves. Encourage them to believe that there is in themselves a mine-pocket full of riches. You can, by your careful and thoughtful training of them, make them wealthy in developed ability.

Countless thousands of men are stranded in business routine. In each one of them may be a latent ability which when developed would be of immeasurable profit to the employer. There seems to be a fatal impression with many businessmen that to hire a man as he is means to keep the man on as he is. But it is wrong to look upon any human being as being irrevocably immovable or unimprovable.

Capital And Labor

BOTH CAPITAL AND LABOR are necessary to society. What poor instruments they are without mutual understanding, trust and faith in each other! What is needed is the growth that will deepen our understanding of each for the other. With it will come the desire for effective action that will result in permanent prosperity for all.

Someone has said, "The greatest resources in the world are not iron, copper or lumber, but human resources. The great need is to strengthen this human foundation. The mind of man is a wonderful thing, but unless the soul of man is awakened, he must lack faith, originality and ambition."

Through the development of the individual soul will come the development of the soul of the nation and the world, bringing with it increasing brotherhood and well-being.

We Admire

WHAT IS IT that we admire in an individual or a business?—
for business is but the reflection of the ideals of an individual.
Is it wealth, position, good looks or beauty, or even pleasant
manners?

No, it is none of these. Many of the men of our nation have
been poor and often downright ugly. Many of our noblest
women have been homely. But through these rough exteriors
has shone that something which has made their names immortal, their lives a blessing and an inspiration to humanity.

What is it, then, that makes the names of people stand out
in our memory? Why, it is that indefinable something called
the soul or spirit! We see an electric light and ask ourselves
what it is. We know it is a power, but it is beyond us to define
it. So it is with that indescribable thing about human beings
which draws us toward them as if by some magnetic power.
Such folks are thoroughly unselfish, courteous, obliging,
sympathetic, charitable, optimistic and hopeful. They see the
good in everything and everybody. They are positive forces
instead of negative. They encourage rather than discourage;
they help instead of hinder; they are full of love instead of
hate.

Thus it is that some people are more popular than others
and some businesses flourish while others dwindle into decay
and fail.

From Sheep To Suit

SOMEONE GRAZES the sheep where they get the best nourishment. Someone clips the wool; someone prepares the wool for the market. Then follow the operations of scouring, cleaning, carding, spinning, and weaving, each one involving human hands backed by human minds. But the process is just begun. The mill distributes the goods to the agent. He in turn passes it on to the clothing manufacturers, and at this point every yard is examined and sponged. It is then ready for the cutter and maker. The product of their skill goes to the retailer, who buys, not from examination of the finished suit, but from a swatch three by five inches.

Back of that little bit of cloth must lie the honor of every individual who has entered into the operation. It is a long way from the grazing of the sheep to submitting the swatch to the retailer. If at any time a single thought of dishonor has entered the production of this suit, the perfect expanding circle has been destroyed.

However humble the task may be, it is part of a long process. Unless that task be well done in relation to the rest, the perfect expanding circle of influence is destroyed.

A Fair Competitor Is A Good Friend

IN A MIDWESTERN STORE of our company we had a young manager afire with ambition to do a good job. One day he heard that another chain planned a new outlet in his community. He wrote our home office for help in his advertising. "We want to blast them and show them the kind of competition they're running into," he said. "We're going to keep our store open until 10 o'clock on the night when the new store opens —and I hope the other merchants will close at 6 o'clock as usual. We'll give them a reception they'll never forget!"

Despite training, this eager young man still labored under the delusion that competition is a dog-eat-dog fight for a limited amount of business, essentially an attitude of the nineteenth century. We wrote back:

"Thank your lucky stars for the coming of another competitor. The more stores, the more business. Welcome them with open arms. We are sending you herewith a heading for your advertising which reads, 'Welcome to Homeville, R. & H. Company. We're glad to have you with us.'

"Incidentally, your staying open the evening of their opening, if all the others are closing, will not only show up your own store as a bad neighbor and an unfriendly competitor but will even fail of its purpose to get business, for you would have to get it alone with no other stores to help bring you customer traffic."

So, I repeat, there is no better friend to any merchant than a fair competitor. Obviously, I do not mean the competitor who starts price wars, uses unscrupulous "bait" advertising, or others of that stripe, but rather the competitor who profits most because he serves best. It is in service that the real competition occurs.

Starting The Day Right

No DOUBT YOU have experienced, as I have, the advantage one has in starting the day right. I have experienced as well the desultory effect of a wrong start. The man who arises refreshed by a good night's sleep, gets to work on time. He has his day's work laid out, as do architects planning a house. He will feel better, be more virile, thoroughly enjoy his work, and in turn radiate happiness to others.

But let this same man have his night's rest broken as a result of dissipation, let him be a few minutes late to work, and the chances are that he will never get caught up. There is a certain psychology in a man's being prompt which fills him with confidence he otherwise cannot experience. He tackles a job, knowing he can do it and determined that he will succeed.

Business Growth

TRADE AND COMMERCE are but an expression of the needs of the human race. Business corporations live and prosper in proportion to their contribution to the needs of the world. Business today is larger than ever before because business men have learned the enormous power of cooperation and the value of good will.

In the old days it was a well-established principle in law that the buyer must beware of any defects in the goods he bought. Today business is getting away from the policy of hiding defects and deceiving people, for it has discovered that the faith and trust of those with whom it deals is its most valuable asset. Where there is confidence there is good business.

Permanent business growth can be acquired only by giving full value in your particular field. As a retail merchant, I learned that the majority of people expect value and recognize it when they get it. And they return for more of the goods that give value. If business men could paste that in their hats, or write it on a card and then set it on their desks, there might be less nonsense about some secret of business success.

There is no secret. Business is an exchange of value. You give products or service, and you get money or its equivalent. In the long run, there is no way to get more by giving less.

Respect Your Business

OTHERS HAVE NO higher regard for our business than we have.
Our regard for it is largely based upon our conception of its
moral inherency. Business must be conducted on the square
to receive our entire support. Right here is found the break-
down point for many a promising concern. Because management knew there was crookedness involved in their methods
of conducting a business, their employees could not come to
it with wholesomeness of mind and enthusiasm of heart.

When a man brings to his daily task the full support of his
moral personality, when he can tell others his problems as he
looks them straight in the eye, when he reaches the heights
of success without being arrogant, when he can look into the
faces of his family and know that they have an honest husband and father, when he possesses the consciousness that permits him to respect himself and compels others to regard him
for his own worth, then is such a man an exponent of business dignity.

Cooperative Competition

AMERICAN FREE ENTERPRISE and cooperation is based upon the idea that the pool of customer wants is almost unlimited. It is not a case of only so much business to be shared among so many merchants, but rather one of expansion of the pool of wants so that all businessmen profit more.

That kind of competition requires cooperating in the staging of events too big for any but the largest firms. It requires interchange of information among competitors, not on their secrets of doing business, but on their methods.

If I were to summarize my views on competition, the list might go something like this:

1. Accept the philosophy of cooperative competition and the idea of an expandable pool of business.

2. Encourage friendly meetings of competitors to discuss and exchange information on matters of mutual interest, such as hours or pricing policies.

3. Welcome new businesses to your community, and make them feel you are *glad* they have come.

4. Organize, if you don't have one, a retail committee in your Chamber of Commerce—or if you have no Chamber, organize that.

5. Do everything possible to attract new competitors to your community.

6. Promote—in every way possible—the business district as a shopping area. The more traffic, the more business.

7. Always remember that you are building not just a business but a community.

What you do every day—and how you get along with your competitor—has everything to do with whether your town will be a bad place in which to live—or a good one.

Man-building

THE MOST VALUABLE and interesting occupation on earth is man-building. This does not mean turning men's minds and bodies into military and industrial machines. It means helping the individual to find that work for which he is best fitted, then developing all his mental and spiritual powers to the end that he looms big in his chosen calling.

All success in business that is enduring and efficient is a result of man-building. Everyone who becomes skilled in the demands of his work and develops his judgment has become a disciple of true and enduring service.

His days will be full of happiness because his is the wonderful privilege of forgetting himself in dedicating his skill to the good of others.

Christian Principles In Business

AT ONE TIME during my business career I broke down, both
nervously and physically, and went to a sanitarium. One night
while there I had an overwhelming conviction that it was
my last night of life. So sure was I that my time had come
that I got up and wrote farewell letters to my family.

The next morning, however, I passed a parlor in the sanitarium and heard singing. A few people were gathered in a
religious meeting. I felt the urge to enter. In great weariness
of spirit I listened to the hymns, to the Scripture reading and
to the prayers. Then, a profound sense of inner release came
over me. A heavy weight seemed lifted from my spirit. I was
amazed at my change, and in the days that followed I regained
mental and bodily health. Perhaps the feeling of death that
night was a symptom of a new man being born in me.

I do not mean to give the impression that because of these
experiences I have successfully applied Christian principles to
all phases of my life. It is true that God has blessed me beyond
what I deserve. Because our company has been conscientious
in practice of the Golden Rule, success has blessed our business. I feel ashamed, however, that in other ways I have not
followed Christ's teachings as well as I might. I have not loved
God as I should. I neglected my obligations to the Church
until recent years. I certainly have not worked for the brotherhood of man outside my business to the degree that should
be expected of a good Christian. But I am now trying earnestly to make up for what I have failed to do in the past.

Those who have the greater part of their adult life before

them should study with great earnestness the relation between Christ's two commandments—to love God and to love
thy neighbor as thyself. With such a balance of these two
great laws worked out in everyday life, there will be a true
measure of spiritual blessing and, I hope, of material prosperity.

Making Haste Slowly

THE GREATEST MISFORTUNE that can befall a man is to be
placed in an advanced position without having earned the
experience below it. Business progress is like climbing a lad-
der. It must be ascended rung by rung.

I know that my own experience has been richer because
I have been associated with individuals who believed in me.
Naturally, a sense of pride compelled me to put forth my
greatest efforts to merit that confidence. At no time in my
life has this appreciation meant more to me than it does
today. Consequently, every minute of my time is employed,
the greater part of it devoted to study in order that I may be
better qualified to assist in meeting the larger problems
incident to a growing program of life.

Choosing Men

THE TYPE OF men we employ is important to the upbuilding of any business, for the success of a store depends on the kind of people who conduct it. The right kind of men increase store business and help others in building up the community of which they are a part.

Men who are attentive to their duties, who do not frequent saloons, who are moral and industrious, are bound to command the respect of all well-meaning citizens. Thus, a man who lives up to our requirements increases his own value, and augments his value to the company.

Our system increases the efficiency of our men by allowing them to participate in the profits according to their ability to get results. This training teaches them economy. Initiative is required of our men in order that they may cultivate judgment which will enable them to see results before steps are taken.

As for the married man, his success depends largely upon the support he receives from his wife. Having studied the question closely for many years, I feel justified in making this statement—a wife can always make or unmake a man. Where a wife is in sympathy with her husband's best interests, she will cooperate with him and she, too, will be thrifty and economical.

The man who succeeds is the man able to analyze himself and his opportunities.

Be Happy In Your Own Job

TUCKED AWAY IN everybody is the conviction that to be able to live somewhere else, to do some other kind of work, in some other circumstance, for some other kind of people, would constitute a happy life. The trouble is that we see the pleasant part of the other person's calling and the disagreeable part of our own.

The fact is that in our own calling there is more happiness than we dream. It is just as true that in the other person's calling there are many difficulties to be overcome, painful moments to be lived, and strenuous tasks to be accomplished. These we do not see.

If a man or woman has not found happiness in work, the probability is that it will never be found anywhere, for happiness lies within. Happiness is not the gift of outer circumstances. The person, be he business man, mechanic, teacher or housewife, who sees and appreciates in his job an unlimited field for self-expression, is at once useful and joyful and has found the Kingdom of Heaven on earth.

Faith Through Trial

I AM FRANK to admit that it took the greatest catastrophe of my life to make me realize the power of God, to learn the meaning of faith and trust, and my duty to Him.

I was absorbed in business to the extent that success to me meant the ceaseless accumulation of money. My desire was to be a wealthy man so that I might some day enjoy the things in life which I thought money could buy.

Finally, like a bolt out of a clear sky, I was struck and awakened. In 1910, the mother of my two older boys died after an illness of brief duration. So sudden and so severe was the shock that it came near to overwhelming me.

Although I never drank liquor, even in moderate amounts, for some reason I now was assailed by an intense desire to drink—perhaps with the unconscious thought of drowning my sorrow. Instinctively, I knew that I must not yield one iota—that if ever that desire got one foot within the door it would come in bodily, and I would come to utter defeat. The desire was persistent and terrible, lasting not only through weeks and months, but even years. Many a night I walked the streets battling with temptation and the darkness that had settled upon me. It was the most difficult time of my life.

If it had not been for the memory of my father's faith in me, I might have faltered and fallen by the wayside. Those are times when inner strength is needed, and must come from somewhere. If it is not forthcoming, then the result may be a tragic one. By understanding the workings of the human mind and spirit, a person is better prepared to face the exigencies of this life. It is this personal understanding of one's self and of the aid God will always give, that help a person to stand alone, if need be, for the things which he has decided count the most.

The Price Of Progress

COOPERATION IS ONE of the great words of the twentieth century. Business men in playing fair with each other have discovered that they play fair with themselves. By working together, by developing harmony, by expanding the trading influence of their town, and by avoiding captious criticism of their neighbors, they multiply their own successes and build the common welfare.

Farmers are cooperating too. They have their associations for studying diversification of crops and scientific marketing. The price of progress is study and hard work, but it is also cooperation with your fellow man.

We Must Sell Freedom!

WE HAVE HEARD too much and too often the expressions
"menial jobs" and "menial work." There are no menial jobs.
There is no menial work. All work, when it is honest, is
honorable. I have never seen any figures on the subject, but I
suspect that fully 90% of all the leaders of American business started their careers in jobs that required manual labor—
proving that manual work and opportunity go together.

The greatest teacher I know is the job itself. Any job—it
doesn't matter what it is. Try listening to it. Hear what it
says. It will tell you if you have done it well or if you haven't.
It will tell everyone else, too.

Ordinary selling, on your part and on my part, is all that is
needed to establish our "merchandise," our American freedom, over the Russian product which is slavery. But, we will
have to do a keep-at-it job of selling.

We aren't very good at plugging, although, as every sales
manager knows, patience earns more commissions than sprint-
ing. It is in our nature to demand results by tomorrow morning, preferably before ten o'clock. We forget that behind
every home run struck by Babe Ruth were ten thousand practice swings.

But, no matter how often we forget that, we must not
forget that Stalin's successors have patience—must not forget
that not a minute in the day passes when the Kremlin is not
scheming our destruction.

That is not my statement. It is based on an order out of

history—an order to Communists, everywhere, from Lenin on down.

It is not very comforting information—that I know. I know, too, that we will have to do a better than 50% job of selling to defeat Communism. But, as free men, we can defeat it—and we will defeat it!—just as we have defeated every enemy that has challenged our freedom.

Freedom is our history. It explains our progress. It insures our future.

Learning Through Mistakes

"A MAN WHO cannot make a mistake cannot make anything." This is undoubtedly true. If a man will profit by his mistakes, he can turn them to good account.

When a man is connected with an organization in which he becomes interested, he soon learns that he must act in harmony with his associates, for without cooperation, organization is impossible. Organization men do not work independently, each in his own place and according to his own ideal, but all work mutually toward the one purpose of the business. This must be a lofty purpose and a clear vision.

Cooperation Brings Results

HERE IS A STORY of worthy competition. A certain town in California is situated on a main road leading to three large and busy shopping areas. One or two of the local merchants had given up in discouragement—and the rest felt pretty hopeless. After all, hadn't they watched the almost daily parade of their own residents toward either one or the other of those shopping areas?

In this situation, the manager of our store first thought the cure for the situation was an appeal to people's home-town loyalties. But sentiment plays very little part in shopping habits; bargains and wider choices do loom important, and there really is no reason why they should be ignored just out of loyalty to one's home town.

The problem concerned every merchant in this little community. How could they cooperate competitively for the vanishing customer's dollar? Our manager then argued that the problem had to be solved by making home-town shopping more attractive.

So the merchants got together, as they so often do, in the retail committee of the Chamber of Commerce and set up a home-town bargain day for each month. Every participant pledged himself to offer some real bargains. Each made his proportionate contribution to the cost of banners, streamers and advertising. The daily paper planned a special edition aimed primarily at the surrounding farms and villages. It was to be a gala day—and every participant, while cooperating with the over-all plan, was competing for the resulting trade. The outcome was truly spectacular. Gains of more than 100 per cent over the previous year were regular occurrences —and gradually the shop-at-home habit became established. Who would not wish to achieve so good a result?

Real Salesmanship

SALESMANSHIP IS LIMITLESS. Our very living is selling. We are all salesmen. A doctor, a minister, or a banker is a salesman. And it has been said that Jesus Christ was the greatest salesman who ever lived. Therefore, all of us should either cultivate or be glad that we possess character, pleasing personality, honesty, sincerity, a helpful attitude, a knowledge of our line, and an untiring willingness, all of which make for successful salesmanship.

Giving A Life

GENERALLY A MAN'S start in business is a combination of circumstances in which the confidence of a friend or trusting employer plays a large part.

It was a lift that the original owners of my first store gave me that started me off. More than any tangible values, more than any money, the faith they seemed to have in me, shoved me forward.

Their confidence was a great asset, and it has been my great example. I have tried to practice the principle ever since. It is really very wonderful what a little responsibility, a little encouragement and a little share of the profits will do for even very ordinary people.

I believe in trusting men, not only once but twice—in giving a failure another chance. When a man has been finally dismissed from one of our organizations, I have always had a sense of personal shortcoming, as though somehow I had not quite measured up. The satisfaction that comes from seeing a misfit making good in new surroundings is one of the real joys of life.

It is a fact, too, that any of us would lose out in some situations. There are many things that I could not do. Because there were men who helped me, who gave me my chance, I found a place that opened new fields of opportunity before me.

Life has no richer reward for any man than the reward that comes with the knowledge that another—a man, or a woman, or a child—has been given a little start toward health, happiness and success by just a little attention or encouragement on our part.

Share!

I WAS FORTUNATE, as a young man, to get employment with a retail store which advertised itself to be responsible to the customer, not in a general way, but in the specific spirit of the Golden Rule. This was to me inspiring. It generated energies and developed talents which I was called upon to exercise when, after an apprenticeship, I was considered worthy to take over the managership of a store. When I was given the privilege of buying a one-third interest in the store, I discovered that management opened responsibilities that I welcomed as a challenge. I began to take count of my new responsibilities, mastering them as I could. As a result of my study, I reached the conviction that I could master them only in accordance with Golden Rule principles I had seen practiced by my father.

Young men today should have similar opportunities to prove and improve themselves. Employers should train them with a view toward partnership participation in the business they help to create. It is my experience that employees will respond to the stimulus of fairness and liberality. Partnership participation makes a man dig into himself to qualify. He becomes eager to master the technique of a job greater than the one he has.

Essentials Of A Successful Career

NOT CLEVERNESS, brilliance or genius, but industry, faith, confidence, and application are the cardinal points in success.

It has been our idea that responsibility develops initiative. In pursuit of this principle, we have always exercised great care in the selection of our employees, from the errand boy up. We have made sure that our material was of the caliber to which responsibility could be transferred. We take care that our men shall be of the highest moral standard and best habits. As soon as they are ready, we shift responsibility onto their shoulders. Responsibility makes or breaks a man. He will either rise to the heights by reason of it, or be crushed by the weight of it. Thus care should be taken that responsibility is not forced on a man before he is ready for it.

Our idea is to transfer responsibility gradually. If you should suddenly give me a one-hundred-pound weight, I could not budge it. But if you started me on twenty-five pounds and then increased it day by day, I would develop to the point where I could lift it. Men gradually trained seldom fail to measure up to each stage. We develop nearly all our own talent by promotion from the inside. Men beginning in the basement know that the road to the presidency is open to them.

The second fundamental on which our business has been built is the idea that a man must be given the opportunity to share in what his labor and initiative create. That is what we have always done, and by the operation of this principle our employee becomes virtually a partner in the business.

By virtue of the faithful application of these two principles, an understanding of and loyalty to the business is developed in our employees from the start. It is this understanding and loyalty which is largely responsible for our success.

There is a false idea that success is to be found only in the great industrial centers. Rather, success is to be found where opportunity is, and that may be in the village quite as well as in the city. There is nothing magical about success. It is simply to recognize opportunity and to develop its fullest possibilities. And opportunity is not out there, tomorrow or next year, but right here and now under one's very nose.

The Soul Of Business

HAS BUSINESS A SOUL? Has it any quality or characteristic by which it lives, thrives, and grows into majestic proportions? If there are things that disrupt and destroy business, there are also things that establish and perpetuate business. These elements are many—industry, frugality, fair-dealing, self-respect, considerateness. But the *soul* of business is confidence.

The Fire Of Sacrifice

JUST AS IT takes the fire to burn the dross from the ore, so does it take the spirit of sacrifice in our lives to bring out the best within us. Trials, labor, grief, are but the fires in our lives which are necessary to purify and bring out our virtues.

In business, sacrifices are demanded of us as well as labor, trials and economies. All these strengthen judgment, make for administrative qualities and cultivate resourcefulness.

Is there any sacrifice worth-while? Yes, because of the compensation. Not the compensation of dollars and cents, or in name and glory, but the compensation to self.

Sacrifice establishes character. It makes for purity of motives, honor, dependability, power for service and unselfishness. It takes the fire of sacrifice to clarify a man's mind and heart so that he can establish the worthier ideals for himself. A man who desires anything must be willing to go the whole way for it, not half way. No man gains anything in the way of power and privileges who does not pay with a change in habits, thought and action.

Successful Organization

A BUSINESS ORGANIZATION should be a group of successful men possessing character, ability and high ideals, and whose purpose is a worthy one. Their efforts, directed with skill plus intelligence, produce the highest average of results to the unit they represent.

The personal factor is the one essential element in the success of any organization. A man in business who does not possess a strong, healthy body and mind cannot succeed.

No man has ever possessed all the necessary qualifications demanded by an organization. Because of its size, an organization requires guidance and care by men who have among themselves an unusual number of superior qualities. There must be superior methods of financing, accounting, buying, distributing, advertising and the like. It is not possible to find all these qualities in a single individual. In an organization, men are selected who are best qualified to fill specific needs. If they prove themselves fully adapted to their lines of work, they become specialists and competent advisors.

III
FAITH, A PERSONAL EXPERIENCE

My Faith Is Not Shaken!

CHANGING WORLD conditions over the decades have not shaken my faith in the ultimate triumph of freedom and justice. I was reared by parents whose faith in God, whose belief that right eventually triumphs, are too deeply implanted in me to doubt the final triumph.

I would, however, emphasize the words "ultimate" and "final." I am not at all sure we may not have to pass through a period of great trial. I am of the opinion that we are in prophetic days, a time when Evil is to be powerful—powerful enough apparently to override the Good.

But we must face conditions as they exist—and possible greater tribulation—as part of the world's destiny, without losing faith that in due time right will triumph over might. A business friend of mine once said that everything tends to make him pessimistic. Our experiences should cause us to examine our faith and re-establish our convictions. We should resolve with God's help to acquit ourselves like men. We should seek and find a deep and abiding faith that cannot be shaken by outward events.

God alone, not evil, is all-powerful. His will for the world is justice and right. Good emerges slowly, but we must not doubt its final victory. God's purpose *will* be established on earth.

A Contagious Faith

I WOULD LIKE to mention certain personal, very sacred matters
which lie close to my heart. Having been blessed with long
life, I have had time to analyze and evaluate the environment
in which I was reared. I am what I am because of early training by my old-school, Baptist-minister father and my loyal,
spiritually-minded mother.

The important fact I wish to emphasize here is that the
faith of my father and mother possessed that vital quality
which made it possible for it to reproduce itself in the lives
of their children and others. That leads me to say that the
final, conclusive test for anybody's faith is whether it is con-
tagious. Dr. Frank Fagerburg expresses this idea when he
says, "What if men dealing with Christian men could note in
a moment that they are not dealing with ordinary businessmen? What if the people next door should begin to see their
neighbors are not just ordinary folks? What if these businessmen, neighbors, workmen, all, would awaken to the fact that
Christian people are extraordinary, honest, pure, clean in
thought and talk, kind, considerate, unselfish, loving?"

As I hark back across the long, busy years I appreciate more
and more the fact that Christian faith animated and governed my father's entire life. Being an old-school Baptist
minister, he preached without remuneration, as was the custom in that church in those days, and supported his family
by farming. Early in life it was impressed upon me that after
all he was a man of but one occupation, that of serving the

Lord. Whether he preached on Sunday, plowed on Monday, sowed on Tuesday, or reaped on Wednesday, it was all to the glory of God.

Pioneers

PIONEERS GIVE MUCH of themselves; pioneering is unselfishness, and unselfishness is Christ-like. It takes courage to pioneer, and courage is an attribute of character as is unselfishness.

A man cannot and will not pioneer unless he is thoroughly unselfish, for he knows when he goes out that others who follow are bound to profit from his efforts. But he does not stop because of this. He has a mission to perform and, in doing his duty, he is strengthened, mentally, morally and spiritually. Hence, pioneers develop rugged characters.

Pioneers are not easily influenced. They give of themselves, but how much more do they get in return! How can we forget those of our fathers, who before the advent of the railroad traveled overland, discovering the Great West. No narrow-minded, selfish individuals would have ventured out from the safety and conveniences of established towns and homes. Pioneers have the spirit to dare and to triumph, through faith in themselves and their God.

Using Spare Time

FAILURES IN BUSINESS are usually the result of a lack of knowledge in business or of insufficient capital with which to finance business.

In my opinion, there is another cause. Many fail simply through lack of training. In Great Britain and Scandinavia, young storemen serve an apprenticeship just as they do in other trades. We find them trained thoroughly, even to the minutest detail. They are taught obedience to discipline; no man can ever hope to become a merchant unless he learns to discipline himself and those who work for him.

In the United States, unfortunately, no apprenticeship system exists in business. The average young man is attracted to, and is free to accept, that position which pays the largest salary. To secure such a position without training is decidedly not for his best interest. Many young men have been ruined by drawing large salaries early in life. The young man is generally eager to see some of the "world" before he settles down. He makes money; he spends it. Instead of devoting his evenings to reading and study to improve his mind, he often spends them in idleness and dissipation. Before long, not only has he acquired bad habits that will be hard to break, but his health may have become impaired.

I have often heard young men argue that if they put in their working time faithfully, it is none of the employer's business what they do outside of business hours. Such argument is nonsense. Any man of experience will declare that it is not the work that kills men, but the temptations that assail them after hours.

The Newspaper

THE CIRCULATION OF daily periodicals has grown by leaps and bounds. One reason for this growth is the fact that families in the country as well as those in town have come to realize that they can find all of their shopping information in the daily press.

The confidence of the public in business houses which carry on consistent advertising campaigns has been developed to a high point by the code of ethics which governs the acceptance of advertising copy. This confidence has been further increased as the larger organizations have become an open book to the population. Their frank publications regarding earnings, sales, volume of business done, personnel and profit sharing have increased the friendliness of the people.

Newspapers could not live today were it not for the revenue which advertising brings. This revenue has made possible armies of news gatherers, and has brought to the reader in the most remote hamlet an intimate glimpse of things which are happening thousands of miles away.

In our generation a liberal education may be obtained by reading the better newspapers. They have become an important adjunct to the daily life of the individual.

The Heroes Of My Own Thinking

IT MAY BE TRUE—and I think it *is* true—that man, as a fallen being, inclines to evil rather than to good. It is easier for him to yield to his passions than it is to heed the voices of self-control. We see examples of human frailty all about us, and within our own lives that record is written. Society itself reflects the weaknesses, the mistakes and the sins of its individual members.

But always there are exceptions to the rule. Always there are men and women who refuse to follow the line of least resistance, who rise above environment, who conquer temptations and who become moral and spiritual leaders of their fellow men. We are all indebted to them and every generation profits by their sacrifices. If I started to name those men and women who qualify for the applause of their fellow men I would run out of the space allotted me here very quickly. They appear in every walk of life and in every area of human activity. They need no eulogy from me; I with you and others are eternally in their debt.

Let me list a few of those who have been the heroes of my own thinking: Galileo, Newton, Franklin, Luther, Calvin, Wesley, Robert Raikes, and Robert Faust. And from these and many others I turn to the incomparable benefactor of the world who is none other than Jesus Christ. He alone is universal. As a human benefactor He alone has served equally, all races, all conditions and all generations since He was born in a Bethlehem manger. He alone is both human and divine, very God and very man. He alone moves across both time and space to open the gate of eternal life and fulfillment to all who follow Him.

The Shining Light

WISE MEN DO not light a candle and place it under a bushel. Life's greatest benefactions—intelligence, liberty, religion— are for dissemination. There can be no moral justification for withholding the benefits that result from a wise distribution of knowledge.

Liberty, that one priceless boon for which all men yearn, thrives only in the light. It must be proclaimed and practiced to be enjoyed and appreciated by all.

Religion was never intended for self-gratification. It must be turned loose upon the world, and the more unconsciously that loosening process takes place, the more beneficial its results.

Christ declared that He was the Light of the world. Religion must scatter that Light or fail in the accomplishment of its supreme mission.

Intercessory Prayer

PRAYER FOR OTHERS, we are told, is more effective than prayer for ourselves. Perhaps this is because there is less of self in our prayer for others. There is no more sacred trust than intercessory prayer. There is no place where subtle powers are more likely to assert themselves. It is easy to pray for what we want; it is far more difficult to pray to know and to do God's will.

The Laymen's Movement for a Christian World issued a Laymen's Call to World Prayer in support of the United Nations. They distributed 800,000 prayer cards and had over 25,000 of these signed and returned. These people volunteered to pray daily that a new spirit, one of good will and cooperation, might be awakened among our world leaders, and that they might be led to do God's will. In addition to urging all to pray, the Laymen's Movement has sent men and women into the daily regular sessions of the General Assembly for the purpose of helping them understand the problems which separate nations, and in order that they may pray silently for those who deliberate. You are cordially invited to join this effort and add your prayers to the prayers of thousands of others who pray daily for a peaceful world society with justice for all. May I recommend a prayer to you? It reads:

"I will try this day to live a simple, sincere and serene life, repelling promptly every thought of discontent, anxiety, discouragement, impurity, self-seeking; cultivating cheerfulness, magnanimity, charity, and the love of holy silence; exercising economy in expenditure, generosity in giving, carefulness in conversation, diligence in appointed service, fidelity to every trust, and a childlike faith in God.

"In particular, I will try to be faithful in those habits of prayer, work, study, physical exercise, eating and sleeping which I believe the Holy Spirit has shown me to be right. Amen."

Personal Development

THE MAJORITY of us are too easily satisfied, especially where personal development is concerned. We are, as a nation, energetic, ambitious and by nature acquisitive; but too many times our business or profession is merely the means to an end, and this is where the mistake is made. If we are in our job because we love it, the financial part of it will take care of itself.

No man can grow in spiritual stature and think continually in the realm of material things. But when he reverses the order and makes the end to fit the means, then he becomes a bigger and better man. Consequently, he develops his personality, which after all is but the expression of the soul.

Knowing God's Will Is Not Easy

AFTER ACHIEVING A fair measure of success in business, I
decided that the "one more thing needed" was for me to learn
how to give myself over to God's purpose. I became convinced that in order to take my faith seriously, I must find
God's will for the use of what talents I possess and that experience I have had. Gradually I have come to realize that knowing God's will is not easy, that one must seek it in humility
through prayer, and that our prayers are often strained
through our own selfish desires and colored by our own wills.
One must keep returning to the Source of all Life in order to
be renewed.

It may surprise you to know that it was not until a few
years ago that I felt I could formally unite with the Church.
There was never a time when I did not believe in the Church
or attend its services. I felt unworthy and, worse still, I was
not willing to do something about it. My responsibility of
church membership came to me very suddenly after I had
spoken in a small Midwest church several years ago. It was
Communion Sunday. I had never taken Communion. What
should I do? I asked the pastor of the church. He said, "Mr.
Penney, why *don't* you take communion?" I replied that I
had always feared I was unworthy. After a few reassuring
words he left me to think it over. As though a Voice were
speaking into my mind, there came the words, gently spoken:
"Don't be afraid!" So, for the first time in my life I partook of
the bread and wine and found it a rich spiritual experience.

Upon my return to New York I arranged for Dr. Daniel

Poling to go with me to the Penney Memorial Home in Florida, and receive me into the church there. The membership of this church is composed of those remarkable retired Christian workers who are spending their sunset years in comfort, peace and quiet there.

Trustworthiness

I BELIEVE a man is better anchored who has a belief in the Supreme Being. His idea in all its details may not be the same as mine, but if he has one that really means something to him, I find that he has a steadiness which other men lack. I find that he has a sense of obligation to his fellow men that other men scorn. I find him trustworthy. My experience teaches me that I can put greater trust in the man who says, "I believe in God . . . and shall love my neighbor as myself," than in a person who says, "I am responsible to no one beyond myself. There is no God."

Our Great Adventure

A FRIEND or mine was packing his bag to attend a Christian layman's retreat. His young son heard him say that he was "making a retreat" that weekend. Knowing best the language of war, the son remarked, "*Retreat,* Dad? Who is after you?"

There is more wisdom in the boy's words than is revealed at first glance. It is not only "who" but "what" is *after* modern man. Our society is extremely complex and very materialistic. In this setting, man struggles to calm his nerves and to develop his spiritual capacities. Nothing can aid him more than to get away from his usual environment to some place where he can think, pray and be silent in the Presence of God.

The idea of a retreat is nothing new. Jesus used it and saw clearly the temptation which faced Him early in His ministry. The saints, Augustine and Francis of Assisi, left their homes to become "grounded in the love of God." George Fox in the first page of his journal says, "I walked abroad in solitary places many days and often took my Bible and sat in hollow trees and lonesome places till night came on." It was in one of these retreats that he made his great discovery: "There is one, even Christ Jesus, who can speak to thy condition."

Today there is even greater need through occasional retreats for us "to let the Spirit of God find its peculiar incarnations in our century—that is our great adventure," says Gilbert Kilpatrick.

We Must Learn To Pray

PRIDE, WHICH TOO often controls us, will not be overcome; neither will the serenity which God is capable of giving us be forthcoming without a more intelligent and persistent effort by each of us to come into, and then to abide in, God's Presence. We must learn to pray.

A remarkable document on prayer was written by Dr. Alexis Carrel, a French doctor and physiologist who died in France during the last war. Listen to his analysis of our predicament:

"To us men of the West, reason seems very superior to intuition. We much prefer intelligence to feeling. Science shines out, while religion is flickering. We seek first of all to develop intelligence in ourselves. As to the non-intellectual activities of the spirit, such as the moral sense, the sense of beauty, *and above all the sense of the holy*—they are almost completely neglected. The atrophy of these fundamental activities makes of the modern man a being spiritually blind. Such an infirmity does not permit him to be an element good for the constitution of society."

Then continuing, Dr. Carrel says, "The fact is, the spiritual shows itself just as indispensable to the success of life as the intellectual and material."

May I say with all humility, "I know that to be true."

Common People May Be Uncommon

IT IS WELL for us to bear in mind that *the glorious success of the early church was primarily due to the pure, irreproachable lives of the common people who comprised its membership.* In those far-off days there were not many church members of high position or education. In spite of this these simple people, without political prestige, lacking in worldly treasure, with no influence as scholars, and sometimes even without friends, separated their neighbors from their age-old allegiance to the ancient gods and the emperor of Rome and made their religion a power in the world. Almost in the beginning hostile government forced them "underground," as we would say today, and many who were unfortunate enough to be ferreted out were doomed to shed their blood in the Coliseum. Church members stood in deadly peril at times, and a host of them died; but the church lived on!

As I recall the soul-stirring fact that these people were Christian in spite of an intensely hostile environment, I ask myself the question, "Shall we Christian laymen of today, living as we do in a land where freedom of religion is a reality, and in a time when nobody threatens us because of our faith, content ourselves with *doing* and *being* less than were our brethren of long ago?"

Do you not agree with me when I say that by every token we ought to surpass them because behind us lies almost two thousand years of Christian thought, achievement and history? In the Western world, at least, men of vast influence and affairs openly confess loyalty to Christ, the church enjoys both

riches and prestige, and the situation in the world today chal-
lenges us to do something about things. And what shall we
do? The only answer I know to that question is, "Be true to
the duty which lies close at hand."

Thirty-five years ago, in the hey-day of his popularity,
Homer Rodeheaver, Billy Sunday's great song leader, taught
the people of America to sing "Brighten the Corner Where
You Are." Those words beautifully express what Christ meant
when He said, "Let your light so shine before men, that they
may see your good works, and glorify your Father which is in
heaven" (Matthew 5:16).

Lest We Forget

IN TIMES OF chastening, we learn once more how to work and
how to live. When life becomes too soft and easy, we forget.
Those of us who have a job and a worth-while future toward
which we can work, may be especially thankful during
anxious times. Let us be generous in extending to others a
helping hand.

Always the future goes forward on the feet of the present,
and the courage with which we march will determine the
character of tomorrow.

The Bible: Our Atom Bomb

SINCE THE DAY shooting ceased with the unconditional surrender of our enemies in Europe and Asia, the councils of the nations—and their efforts to usher in an era of peace—have been frustrated by a world power dedicated to the principles and extension of Communism through the world. A bridgehead has been established in our midst under the name of the Communist Party of the United States, a group whose self-expressed aim is the violent overthrow of our government, democracy and religion.

Although these people constitute only a small minority of our population, the threat they pose to our way of life is considerable. How then shall we counteract and nullify this foreign ideology? Not with guns, nor even the atom bomb, for such ideas cannot be conquered by military might. The only effective weapons for such a struggle must be drawn from our spiritual armory, so to speak. The Bible is the answer to Karl Marx's Communist Manifesto, and religion the only power on earth strong enough to defeat Communism.

Therefore our responsibility is clear and our task outlined for us. Teach the Bible in season and out of season, bring its holy, purifying, ennobling influence to bear upon every boy and girl in our land, strengthen our churches, prove to the world that our religion is a source of strength, righteousness and power.

IV
FAMILY AND YOUNG PEOPLE

Laws Of Success

ADVERTISING PLAYS AN important part in the building of any business. There are many ways of advertising: by circular, by newspaper and by word of mouth.

In circular and newspaper advertising, the copy should contain no exaggerated statements and no reference to competitors. In what we call word-of-mouth advertising, every reference should be exact. A satisfied customer is the greatest asset of any business.

A few years ago I stopped at a hotel where the service was the best I had ever known. Behind the desk of each employee, but hidden from public view, hangs a sign with these words, "My reputation is in your hands." How true it is of any organization. Your employer's business, his reputation and your reputation—all are in your hands. Are you expecting the best today, or are you attracting the worst things by anticipating them? Have you the bulldog grip which never lets go? Have you the grit which pushes on when everybody else gives up? If you have not, your employer is headed for disappointment and you are in pursuit of failure. The laws of success are just as surely written as the old laws of the Medes and Persians.

Allied Youth And Its Work

ALLIED YOUTH IS A non-political and non-denominational organization, dedicated to the task of helping our high-school youth become emotionally mature, so that they will not run away from their problems or seek artificial means of escape. It utilizes the best of modern guidance materials in its work, and is endorsed by leading citizens and educators throughout the country. Significantly, for three successive years Allied Youth received the Freedom Foundation Award in recognition of its outstanding youth conservation program.

It is my hope that you have gained a clearer understanding of the vital job that Allied Youth is doing in the realm of human relations, for the test of the individual and his greatness is not the magnitude of the problems he faces, but how well he adjusts himself to the conditions in which he finds himself, and solves those problems. The matter of adjustment is a complex one, and one never finds a simple answer that will cover all the decisions he must make. Not every young person secures for himself the happiness and well-being which can be his lot. Many a youth, through insecurity, feelings of inferiority, worry, or just plain lack of knowledge, falls into a pattern of living that has no goals or hope for the future.

That is why I consider so important the work of Allied Youth. It provides that self-knowledge for young people which, educators tell us, best insures that one can expect an enjoyable and worth-while life.

Rules Of Success For Young People

JUST AS A young man is loyal to and thorough in his work, so is his increasing success certain. Nothing can turn years of carelessness into years of fruitfulness.

No man can be a great success who does not make it a practice to be on time. We should be as honest with time as with money.

Experience teaches the absolute necessity for carefulness. Training in carefulness develops an individual and makes him well poised. Be careful of the body. A clean and healthy body attracts favorable attention and enables a man to do better work.

Learn to dress neatly. You will not only present a superior appearance, but establish confidence in yourself.

Honesty and truthfulness are the best policy, and they have their own compensation. The "let the buyer beware" theory is no longer the accepted way. Fair and just treatment, truthful statements in selling talk and advertising get and hold business.

Growth

FUTURE DEVELOPMENT in a man depends greatly upon his early training. We should emphasize the beginning of a career because the beginning is the foundation of everything worthwhile.

Nature has allotted to each of us twenty-four hours a day to be spent as we see fit. The day is usually divided into three parts: eight hours for work, eight hours for recreation, and eight for sleep.

In the case of many a man the day is divided in two unequal parts: sixteen hours for labor, and eight hours for sleep. Very often the division is even more unequal than this. There was a period when my own life was very disproportionately divided, for I did not think it necessary to devote any attention to recreation and often I did not get eight hours sleep. I am sure that I was very unwise. Our bodies are not mere machines and should not be treated as such.

It is not only how the time is divided, but how it is employed. The man who is the most systematic in the handling of his time will be the most successful. A person must analyze himself, and select a career for which he is adapted. Then, he should identify himself with a going concern, in which he may receive a thorough training and an opportunity to advance.

Let him then submit himself to the most rigid discipline. No man can succeed who does not know what discipline means. He must study, too—long and deeply—and never get beyond the stage of looking for new ideas and searching for better plans.

A Christmas Message

THE STORY OF the Babe in the manger, the star of Bethlehem, and the three wise men is old but ever new. One cannot think of it without being struck with the rare beauty and simplicity of it all. Yet, there is sometimes a tendency to overlook the deep religious significance of Christ's birth in the frenzy of gift-giving.

Christmas in the home should be more than just a time for festivity and merrymaking. It is a time for the contemplation of eternal things, for teaching the children fundamentals of God's love in sending His Son to earth.

Therefore, we should make the Yuletide season an occasion for the giving of more than material things. Give that which counts infinitely more—give of yourself.

Woman, A Real Partner

EVERY MAN RETAINS vivid memories of his first "location"—
not perhaps the place of his first job, but the farm or town
where he went into business for himself. The opportunity
may have been small, full of risks and hard work; but if it
was the beginning of a career, it remains in his mind to bring
back grateful recollections.

My wife and I came to the little store in Kemmerer,
Wyoming, with our first son and $500—all that we had been
able to save. We moved into the one low-ceilinged attic room
above the place where we carried on our business. It was
hardly a room. Light filtered through a small window; there
were store boxes for chairs and these, with a table, provided
the only furniture.

My wife helped me in the business. We worked until late
at night. When the second baby came, she would often wrap
him in a blanket and make a bed for him on one of the
counters. After the long hours I have watched her bathe the
children in that little room.

The town had only a thousand people; but as I look back
to my days in it, there is a sense in which it stands higher in
my thought than all the cities that I have visited since.

If I could find a word to help another young man and
woman who are beginning their life together I should be very
happy. I know that whether great success comes or not, the
feeling of having met a situation, of having tried to build a
home and a business honestly on firm foundations, is worth
more than millions.

Often since those days, I have said it was the partnership, the partnership with the mother of my boys, the work with her by my side, that gave me hope, that kept me going. And it is this partnership in the home, on the farm, in the shop, everywhere, that makes for success today.

Young People

CAREFUL OBSERVATION of youth under all conditions does not make me feel that young men and women of this generation are any worse than those of other generations. Certainly we are living in a faster time, and many are making sad mistakes. But, as to drinking and the rest, I am quite convinced that there is more "noise" than the actual conditions warrant. As far back as I can remember, some adults have decried the excesses of the younger generations and have insisted that youth were not what they had been when *they* were young. We who are older need good memories.

It is my candid opinion that young folks do not act worse now than their elders. Generally, they reflect the examples, good and bad, that are set before them.

The Importance Of Reading

THE READING OF good books is one of the most helpful ways in which young people can develop themselves. One of the saddest mistakes I made in years gone by was utter neglect of reading. I realize now what I have missed by not having read and studied more.

I should like to say to the young men in particular that it is a splendid thing to make money, but it is a greater thing to make a good way of life. If they will devote some time each day to reading the best books they can find they will derive a lasting benefit throughout their lives.

To read good books casually will not suffice. One must study every sentence and make sure of its full message. Good writers do not intend that we should get their full meaning without effort. They expect us to dig just as one is compelled to dig for gold. Gold, you know, is not generally found in large openings, but in tiny veins. The ore must be subjected to a white heat in order to get the pure gold. So remember this when you read.

Young men and women who are seeking to learn all they can, have minds capable of receiving and retaining new impressions. There is nothing that will strengthen the mind, broaden the vision, enrich the soul, like the reading of good books. One can find or make no better friend than a good book.

Education Is An Investment

I HAVE LONG believed in education as an inspiration for the continued unfolding of mental powers which should go on all through life. When I am told that a man is seriously studying his work to perfect himself in it and to discover its greater possibilities, I am sure that he has found the secret of advancement. Such a man will make his way and be heard from as the years reveal the secrets that are to be discovered through patient and well-directed inquiry of an educational nature.

A man must seriously study his work if he desires to go forward into more responsible places. And advancement is not the only reward that will come to him. With the unfolding of the mind, life will be enriched and the world about him will reveal more avenues along which he may travel in quest of that opportunity for helpfulness which is the spirit of all true service.

"Let George Do It"

IT IS SAID, and often accepted, that young people today are yet another disillusioned generation. War after war makes them feel that the world is in a bad way—that there is nothing to be gained by individual effort and ambition. And that is understandable, but—it isn't true! There is much to be gained, both in personal satisfactions, and for the good of our country as a whole, in returning to the rugged American codes that put the responsibility for each man's success on his own shoulders.

I don't know, frankly, how deep this disillusionment goes. What I do know is that young men gave wonderful accounts of themselves in Europe and in Asia, risking their lives with the same fervor and all-out devotion that has been true throughout our history. In school, they risk their necks on football fields, and their legs on baseball diamonds. We have all the proof we need that the American spirit is as sturdy today as it ever was.

But somehow, it has also been invaded by an idea of "Let George do it"—when it comes to setting up the patterns of everyday life. Let me give you an example:

The son of a family friend came to see me about getting a job. On such occasions, I try, always, to find out something about the person, to get the feeling of his attitude toward life and work and his future.

But I could sense that he had definite questions on his mind—he wasn't interested in hearing me talk about starting at the bottom and building a career. Though he'd probably be the last to admit it, what he wanted to know was—"What's in it for me? What can I get out of a job?"

I gave him an opening to ask his first question—and what do you suppose it was? He asked whether we had a pension plan!

The Family Tree

FRANKLY, I HAVE no patience with the fellow who is forever boasting of his ancestors, talking about his family tree. I agree with one of the most distinguished of Americans who said some time ago that family trees are all right, but they need "constant spraying." When we fall back upon family reputation, or make capital out of the success of our ancestors, frequently we are trying to excuse our own failure or are looking for an alibi.

Just the same I do believe in having pride in one's forebears and parents, a pride that gives us a sense of gratitude for their sacrifice and early training, and that sends us on to honor their memory by becoming responsible, successful citizens and earnest Christians.

What Is Past Is Prologue

WHAT WILL OUR youth, the boys and girls of today, do when they take over this nation, this world of ours, tomorrow? If the fear of the unknown is frightening to us older folks who have faced and conquered many such fears, what type of tensions and trembling must these young folk feel when they face the problems of an atomic age not yet tested by any man? Indeed, they must often wonder how they will bear up under fire.

However, this prospect of days to come should not give us cause for great alarm. We have some yardsticks to help us gauge how today's youth will later measure up to their tasks and responsibilities. There is great truth in the motto emblazoned on the Archives of the United States: "What is Past is Prologue." In this building in our nation's capital, which houses the historic documents and relics of our heritage, we can indeed find clues to how our youth will respond to adversity in the future. If we comb the events of the past, we can rediscover those principles upon which national and individual greatness are based, and from which integrity grows. These principles are largely ones which must be applied by the individual in his own life, but the collective action of all its citizens is reflected in a nation's outlook and achievements.

Now Is The Time!

HAVE YOU EVER heard a man say that he was looking for the chance to show what he could do, that all he needed was an opportunity to make good? This is a dangerous attitude to assume toward life, an almost fatal policy wherever practiced. The young artist who is never satisfied with his part will very likely continue to be an understudy.

Life, like the fountain of Ammon, overflows only at dawn and during the early morning. Take advantage of the time of overflow. As in the springtime life takes on its season's color, be sure that your life gets anew its form and coloring for a beautiful manhood or womanhood and a serene old age. Let the weeds get the start of the farmer, and he is bound to be the slave of weeds. Those who allow no weeds to crowd into the heart and mind, have a reasonable hope for a happy and prosperous life.

Does Youth Want Security
Or Opportunity?

THE YOUNG MAN who came to me to inquire about a position—
whose first question was "Have you a pension plan?"—in-
trigued me. Now that's an odd beginning, I thought. So I
asked him why a pension plan seemed so important to him.

"Well," he said, "I understand from what I've heard and
read that unless a company has a retirement plan, it isn't a
good place to work."

The thing that disturbed me most was the implication that
he would automatically expect the company he worked for
to make provision for his future, rather than that he under-
take to make it for himself.

So I tried another tack. "What about a new company—
one that has just started, and hasn't been able to set up a retirement plan?" I was thinking, you see, of my own small
beginnings in business, and the men who staked their time,
their labor, and their careers on what they could contribute
to the success of the business.

This was his answer: "I just wouldn't work in a place like
that. Suppose I started there, spent two or three years with it,
and then the company went bust. Where would that leave
me?"

He had no idea at all that his own conscientious contribution, in work, interest, and ideas, might help start the company on its way to a success in which he would share.

"In other words," I said to him, "all you are looking for is security?"

He agreed.

"But what about opportunity?" I asked him.

He appeared to think that was up to the company, too. If the company was big enough and strong enough, it would provide the opportunity for his future success.

"Has it occurred to you," I asked him, "that any opportunity, any participation in a retirement plan, has to be worked for and earned?"

Do You Want An Education?

As TO AN education, the first question I would ask any boy or girl is not, "What advantages and facilities do you have?" but "How much do you want an education?" May I say frankly to you young people that unless you are possessed of a burning, consuming desire to obtain knowledge, no matter where or how long you may go to school, you will never become a truly educated person.

The difference between an educated and uneducated person is not explained by a difference in advantages, but in the will to do. You may boast of the most beautiful, up-to-date school building in the world and the most complete equipment, but unless you apply yourself earnestly to your studies and improve your opportunities, the equipment will do you no good and the building will be nothing more than a pleasant place in which to spend time. It is *your* work that counts!

Who Will Start At The Bottom?

A YOUNG MAN came to me looking for a possible position with
our company.

Not wishing to say an absolute "no," I said there might be
a job for him in one of our stores, and suggested that he talk
with someone in the Personnel Department.

"What would I do in a store?" he asked, looking doubtful.

So I told him—and the story was exactly the same as it has
been throughout the history of retailing, and, indeed, of any
business where a beginner makes his beginning.

"Since you are a green hand," I said, "the store manager
would start you in hustling stock, sweeping and scrubbing
floors, washing windows, and, in your spare time, he would
train you to be a merchant. That is, of course, if you get a
job."

He shook his head. "I want a job in the advertising department, writing advertising copy," he said, and when I pointed
out that he would need merchandising experience to do that,
he assured me he could "pick up the merchandising lingo in
no time at all, and nobody would know the difference."

Two things, I am sure, stand in the way of this young man.
It was obvious that he had no intention of working with his
hands, from the look of distaste when he learned what would
be required of him in a store, and it was apparent he had no
intention of starting at the bottom.

Over the years I have talked with a great many young
people. They used to be pretty willing, generally speaking,

to start at the bottom; and they did not mind if the work was dirty, or hard, or the hours long. What they wanted was opportunity. At least, that is my best recollection of my impressions of talks with them.

This is too often not true today. Too many young people seem to want to be executives from the minute they start, and preferably with telephones on their desks, buzzers within handy reach and secretaries at their elbows—with pension plans neatly wrapped up awaiting their retirement from business.

Caring For Children

PARENTS SHOULD EXERCISE great care in directing their children toward a life work. Advice, counsel and even admonition from parents to child, all have their place; but never should there be coercion into a life work. As fully as possible, the child should be fitted by educational advantages to adjust himself or herself to the normal activities and occupations of life. When this had been done, the child should be permitted to move toward that undertaking in which he feels the thrill of pride and into which he will bring all the enthusiasm of his soul.

Building A Man

"As THE TWIG is bent so is the tree inclined." For this reason we must go back to early childhood to start to build our man, or as Dr. Holmes says, we must pick out a good grandfather for him. The early impressions, the forming of right habits, the inheritance of right tendencies, the influence of the home and parents, and proper associations have great bearing on the life of any man.

A child should be taught, first, the value of character. Reputation is made later on in life, but character is formed in childhood by doing the correct thing in the correct way. He should be taught how to develop himself physically, for a strong mind has difficulty in dwelling in a sickly body.

A child's school days have great influence on his later life, for it is then that the life foundation is laid. If he has learned to think clearly, and judge fairly, he has a good start in life. And he should learn early the habit of economy.

Taking for granted that up to twenty-one a young man has had the proper training, he is then ready to build. He who has learned the value of character, of physical fitness, of economy and thrift, has mastered the lessons which will stand him in good stead and give him a decided advantage over his brother who is less soundly prepared.

Beginning Right Is Better

YOUTH IS THE time of beginnings. It is so much better to begin
right than to begin wrong and then attempt to change. It is
always easier to prevent an evil than it is to make a cure.

I have seen men who had been warned repeatedly by little
signs that told them they should take a rest, work themselves
into nervous prostration. A few days would have set them
right. A brief trip would have restored them to good health.
Eventually they spent months in a sanitarium, away from
their families, away from the office and at the end of these
months they found themselves still far short of what they
used to be.

Of course, the principle applies morally as well as physically, and to governments as well as to individuals. It is easier
for us to observe a law than it is for the police to enforce a
law against one of us who breaks it.

Book Learning Is Only A Part Of It

WHY IS IT that so many young people today are unwilling to start at the bottom and work with their hands?

Perhaps it is because there is something lacking in our system of training. In the home, there is too much pride in giving our children the best possible education; in school there is too much reverence for books, too little for practical living; in our daily contacts, there is too much genuflecting to position and too little consideration given to capability. We seem to be forgetting that when the mind is educated, and the hand is left ignorant, the person is but half trained.

Right here I want to say I am not belittling books, nor book education. To do that would be foolish. I know. From the time I finished school I was not much of a reader. I really had no time, so I thought, for anything so unproductive and inactive as reading. Then, one day in New York, after I was well established in business, I dropped into the show room of a book concern which had space on the same floor with our offices.

I was curious about how books sold and as I was talking with the manager I picked up a volume written by a man named Thomas Tapper. It was entitled "Youth and Opportunity." More out of appreciation for the bookseller's courtesy than anything else, I bought the book, and having paid for it, figured I ought to get something for my money. So I read it.

The book made such an impression on me that I arranged to meet the author and proposed that he take me in hand and tutor me. For eighteen months I worked half of every business day, reading and writing under Dr. Tapper's direction. Nothing was permitted to break up our appointments. One of my most fixed habits at the time was store visiting, but throughout those eighteen months I hardly went out on the road. Those months were among the richest and most stimulating of my life.

I got to know authors from Plato to Thackeray to Ruskin, and I am more grateful than I can tell you for the introductions to these gifted men. But, whatever the genius of such men, or such American authors as Poe, Emerson, Hawthorne and Longfellow, it is well for us to keep in mind that the pioneers who built our country were, for the most part, men of little book learning; and, to remember it is the skill of the mechanic that makes possible—to a very considerable extent!—our standard of living.

Optimism

IN THESE DAYS we need optimism. Not the thoughtless variety that sets up the visionary in place of what should be the true vision. But the optimism that goes at the job, whatever it may be, in the conviction that it can be done well, that it can be made to contribute to the general good, and, that in itself, a job well done is an amazingly powerful thing.

How To Be A Leader

THE YOUNG MAN who can answer these questions has made a promising start on the road to success:

1. Where am I going to be when thirty-five? Fifty? Sixty?

2. Am I doing anything other than my routine work to qualify myself to fit a responsible position at that time?

3. Am I using my spare time in a way that is going to improve me so that I shall be a more valuable, better-rounded, better-trained business man ten years hence?

4. Am I taking a reasonable amount of the right kind of exercise to keep me physically fit for the work I contemplate undertaking?

5. Are my habits and mode of living such that I shall build up a strong, healthy body and a keen vigorous mind?

6. Have I enough self-control and power of will to undergo the self-sacrifice that my ambitions entail? To save sufficiently for the educational courses or other equipment needful to educate myself properly? Have I thrift enough to accumulate the capital required for business enterprise?

The Loyal Man

A MAN, to be a patriot, must be loyal to God, country, family and friends. Loyalty commands the profound respect of all law-abiding citizens. A loyal man is self-sacrificing and thoroughly unselfish. The loyal man is courageous and his convictions are born of high ideals. He has a standard by which he is guided, and he speaks the truth openly, for he has nothing to fear. He is honorable in his dealings. He is sympathetic in his relations to others, and he discharges his obligations as if his very life depended on them. The loyal man cannot be bought.

In business one finds his channel for personal expression, and just as surely as a woodsman is known by his chips, so is a businessman known by the conduct of his business.

Christian Endeavor

I HAVE HAD the privilege of attending International Christian Endeavor Conventions through the years. Perhaps it is the fellowship of this young people's movement that has impressed me. In this organization, young men and women of all races, colors and creeds come together for a common purpose. It is possible for them to mingle without raising misunderstandings, and in so meeting they have contributed in a remarkable way to better relationships among peoples.

I do not know of any agency that has a more important future in promoting world peace than Christian Endeavor. Youth who are not disillusioned and cynical, who believe ardently in the principles of the Prince of Peace, who are always ready to attempt the impossible, give us our best hope for the outlawing of war. I have always been interested in international relationships and in those enterprises which make for good will. More and more I have come to realize how many natural prejudices must be overcome before the goal can be reached. But as I catch the inspiration of a great Christian youth movement, the future seems full of promise.

V
PERSONAL REMINISCENCES

We Change With The Years

I ALWAYS LOOKED forward from year to year to the County Fair. I was thoroughly interested in everything that went on. In the center of the half-mile country track was a pond upon which I, as a lad, had skated in winter. One of the surprises of my life came when I returned to the fair grounds after thirty-five years and discovered that the pond was no longer the great lake that I had remembered it to be.

As I became familiar with the surroundings, I realized that the pond had not changed at all. Rather, it was I who had changed. Of course the surroundings had altered too. The horses and buggies were gone. Automobiles had taken their place. But the change within my own life was greatest. It had affected my view of almost everything else.

How glad I was to find that some things were still the same. All about me were little boys who were still as interested in the events as I used to be, who thrilled to the balloon ascension as I had, nearly two generations before. In their excitement and joy, I had compensation for the altering years, realizing after all that we find our chief satisfaction in others.

Watermelons

Is THERE A BOY anywhere in America who has never tried to grow watermelons?

My first experience nearly ended in the midnight raids that stripped my vines. I say "nearly," for I finally took my dog and slept in the patch. I have found since that there are many times when a man must follow the same principle in business affairs. Business is a day and night assignment, particularly in some of its first stages. The clerk who watches the clock and who crowds his dinner hour to the last minute will likely lose a good many watermelons!

I remember an occasion when I hurried off to a ball game before I had finished the churning. I conceived the bright idea of plastering butter from the pantry around the rim of the churn to convince the family that the work had been well done. Though I failed in my duty with the churn dasher, Father did not fail to do his duty—use the cherry stick!

We are very much inclined to look upon discipline as a hard word. As parents we frequently pity our children to such an extent that we take away from them the sterner experiences we may have passed through and out of which we may have come with deep convictions that have enabled us to meet successfully the grave difficulties everyone is bound to face in life.

Discipline may be a hard word, but it is a hopeful word too. I cannot imagine any real success without a background of discipline.

Fourth Of July

FOR ME AS A BOY the Fourth of July was very much the same from year to year. There was little money to spend on fireworks. If the family had one bunch of firecrackers, it was a great event. Each member of the household watched most carefully to see that every cracker went off. Even the town as a whole could not afford to make much of the anniversary. About four in the morning on the Fourth, the blacksmith in the village would put powder in the anvil and the explosions that were produced made our celebration.

The Fourth of July, as the anniversary of the nation's birth, has grown upon me. I am glad that now it has less noise and more of the deep emotions that prompt us to revere the patriots who purchased our freedom, and to honor the public servants who have enriched our national life.

The Fourth of July, to be properly celebrated, must be more than an explosion of powder and a flare of lights. It must be a time of dedication to the ideals of our free government and to the purposes of universal brotherhood.

Self-assertion Is Necessary

IN MY first job, when I was beginning as a salesman, two men delighted in teasing me about the clothes I wore, the wages I was getting, and anything else that occurred to them as a subject for ridicule. When I had a customer, one or the other would come and take him away on a pretense such as, "I am afraid you will miss the sale." I became discouraged; I shrank into myself and kept away from them, for I was very sensitive to their gibes. However, I did not loaf on the job; I busied myself with arranging stock and took great pride in keeping it in good shape. But I was not happy; I was getting nowhere, either financially or otherwise.

One day something happened within me. To this day I cannot account for it. If I were in that store now I could go directly to the spot where this change took place. Unbidden, the spirit of self-assertion flamed within me. "Jim Penney," said this new spirit, "you are making a fool of yourself; you are getting nowhere. The end of the year will roll around. The owner will say, 'Jimmy, I can pay you but little more; your sales don't show up very well; I'll give you $50 for the year if you want to sign up to run errands and do chores.'"

That was not at all what I wanted to do. Then and there I resolved that henceforth I was going to assert myself and that neither the salesmen nor anyone else could hold me back.

That was the turning point of my early life, for I carried out my resolve. I stood my ground firmly, would not allow the salesmen to take away my customers, and exerted every effort to make sales. By the end of the year I was third in sales.

My First Speech

I DO NOT remember when I first began speaking at church and school affairs, but I am afraid that I was a bit vainglorious. When I was a child I announced that I intended to be a preacher. I can remember how I put my hands behind my back and made a pretense of reading from the Bible, trying to do what I had seen my father do.

Years later at a meeting, I so mixed my notes that I became embarrassed beyond the point of recovery. I floundered about hopelessly, talking completely at random, and felt utterly humiliated at the outcome.

I could not allow that experience to end the matter. I realized that public speaking was not only an art, but that it was an ordeal as well. I would have to pay the price for success here as in merchandising. Once again I learned that all things come to those who wait—provided they "hustle" while they wait.

What My Parents Left Me

MY PARENTS left me little of this world's goods, but their inspirational heritage is mine to enjoy. I would not exchange it for all the material wealth they could possibly have left me. I feel that in a way the prayers of my good mother and the kindly benediction of my father are being fulfilled.

Our lives are made up and are a part of all that we see, read, and hear spoken. Each individual exerts an influence over his fellow man. It is necessary, therefore, if we would have it far-reaching, that we live that kind of life that will be worthy of emulation. Children often follow the example set for them by their parents. Much depends on the home environment and early scholastic training. If a child is taught the importance of truthfulness, obedience, integrity, and if he is instructed in habits of thrift, economy and industry, by the time he has attained his majority he has a good foundation to build on.

Some folks think their children will come out all right, and leave them to grow as Topsy did. But disappointment is bound to be the result. You would wonder about a farmer who expected to gather a crop from land that had not been properly tilled or in which no seed had been planted. You would not expect to gather figs from thorns, nor grapes from thistles. Likewise, a child will not develop into a useful man or woman without careful training.

The True Christian Life

MY FATHER was an old-fashioned, hard-shelled Baptist preacher. Very often I speak of him and even more often my thoughts return to him and to my mother. His faith was simple but it had power.

My father believed in fasting, and he had faith in prayer. Today I believe that only through fasting and prayer can mankind realize the peace of God. His teachings require us to be diligent in prayer and to have a definite objective in our spiritual life. We must have a full realization, too, that (natural) science can never replace the benefit of spiritual, religious, and moral attitudes. We can accomplish more in this world by a true love of God and our fellow man than by any natural or materialistic development. Humility, with confidence in God, is a primary requisite for sound success. Our daily lives must be consistent with our prayer life. Without this constancy we may not enjoy the spiritual heritage of the past. This heritage is vital to our democratic way of life.

A Pig In A Pen

MY FATHER was an old-school Baptist preacher who served his people without pay. His farm was his only income. He was a good stockman, not satisfied with mediocre animals. He fed beef cattle and raised draft horses and carried on both operations successfully.

I was born and reared in this environment, and was brought up in a very strict fashion, being taught early in life not only the nobility of labor, but the necessity of it. He always discussed animals with me, and while about his work, would call my attention to little things which I have never forgotten. I know now that it was his method of teaching me what he knew.

When I was eight years old, it became necessary for me to provide my own clothes. What a shock this information from my father was! I knew that he meant it, that there could be no appeal, for I knew him; and so I counted my pennies. I found that I had exactly two dollars and fifty cents. I bought a little Berkshire pig with the money, and built a pen for him in the back yard.

Although our farm was two and one-half miles from Hamilton, Mo., we had moved into a little town house in order that we might have school advantages. I was given permission to go out to the farm on Saturday and to follow after the huskers. I picked up the ears of corn that were left behind and fed

them to my pig; also, with a pail, I made the rounds of the
neighbors' back doors and gathered in the slops.

In the fall I made a sale and bought more pigs. By bargain-
ing and trading, I increased my drove until I had eleven. I
fed them carefully through the winter, with the idea of selling
in the autumn, when they would bring the best price. Alas,
I was doomed to disappointment.

The pig-pen is an unpleasant neighbor during the hot
summer months. When August came, this fact was brought
to my attention by complaints received by my father. I had to
sell the pigs. I protested, of course, knowing that my pigs
were not in good condition. Autumn was the time to sell pigs.
But Father said, "Sell!" and so I drove them up-town and got
for them what I could.

You may imagine that this experience was a bitter one, but
it did not discourage me. I know now that it made a real contribution to my life. I grew to like farming and trading.

Hard things do not necessarily discourage young people,
but always the young must feel that they are doing something.
This experience taught me to be a bit more resourceful.

Always I shall be grateful to my stern parent for the hard
schooling he gave me. He taught me more than a lesson—he
gave me a true picture of life.

A Good Neighbor

IN REFLECTING on my experience as a raiser of hogs, I realize
I learned another valuable lesson: that of being a good neighbor. For some reason, our neighbors objected to the raucous
squealing that went up every feeding time. Thus, Father told
me that although he would like to see me carry on in the
business, the neighbors were protesting, and so I must sell
the pigs. It was useless to protest, and in obeying my father,
I learned how to be a good neighbor.

These early experiences illustrate how it is possible for a
boy to grow up to be moral and upright, join and attend
church with some regularity and support worthy causes, and
still not attain fullness of life. Don't misunderstand me. The
above-mentioned practices are all worthy and are associated
with one's being a Christian, but they do not go far enough.
They take for granted that a man is spiritually awake and
growing in his understanding of God's spiritual laws.

I am reminded of the experience which Jesus' disciples
had with the boy whose father brought him to be healed.
They tried but failed. When Jesus came and healed the son,
He told them why they could not cure the boy saying, "This
kind of evil spirit comes out only by fasting and prayer."

Christmas

IN MY OLD HOME we eagerly looked forward to Christmas. We always felt the spirit of the day and were always happy with each other. I sometimes wonder about it now. I am almost afraid for children—they have so much that there seems little left for them to anticipate or really enjoy.

I believed in Santa Claus, believed even when older boys laughed at me for my faith. We had no fireplace, only a wood stove, and I could not figure out just how the wonderful old gentleman got in, but I was sure that he did, nevertheless. The fact that I believed in him took care of the details. Contrary to present-day argument, this faith did not affect my later life unfavorably. When I discovered that Santa Claus was a disembodied spirit, all was well. My deeper faith in God and Jesus was not destroyed.

Indeed, I am glad that I had this childhood thrill and vivid experience. It has blessed me all these years.

I Remember

ONE OF THE most vivid and painful recollections of my life is the memory of the day my father was "excommunicated" from his church. What it meant to all of us can never be told, but in this experience my father became a finer Christian and a greater man than he had ever been before. It was his refusal to become embittered, his willingness to bear the cross of misunderstanding, and his example before us that saved me from becoming a cynic with regard to Christianity.

What was it that caused him to be excommunicated? My readers will be amazed when I say that it was his advocacy of what would now be called "Christian education"—his demand for Sunday schools and Bible instruction with his determined appeal for a salaried minister. He lived in advance of his times among the people of the church with which he was associated, the Primitive Baptist.

I want to pay tribute not only to the fearless parent who left upon my life an influence I could never escape, but my expression of profound gratitude for all that Sunday school training and instruction have meant to the life of the world. I have watched the increasing efficiency and ever advancing scholarship of the Sunday school program. I believe in these great conventions and I hope the time will never come when we lose sight of the place of inspiration and fellowship which have played so large a part in Sunday school progress.

Practical Application Of
The Golden Rule

I WAS twenty years old when my father died. At that time I was quite unaware of the training he had given me. Let me give you one example of his teaching—an illustration which becomes more meaningful with each passing year. It is simply a practical application of the Golden Rule in one's own business dealings.

When a boy of 12, I took a load of watermelons to the county fair. Finding a good spot outside the gate, I proceeded with unusual success to sell my product. Just then my father came by and ordered me home.

Later he said, "Jim, do you think I will permit you to sell those melons outside the gate when men have paid for concessions to sell them inside?" At this time I could not have told you that this was a practical application of the Golden Rule. You might say standards such as this one were latent within me. It was not until many years later, at a critical crossroad in my life, that I began to get an insight into the real meaning of this rule and of the many others which Christ laid down some 2,000 years ago.

A Tribute To My Mother

OF MY many recollections of my mother's beautiful spirit, perhaps the foremost is of her patience and next of her unselfishness. Occasionally some friend or neighbor meeting me on the street would give me a stick of candy which I took home. After it was divided, Mother's share was placed on the clock shelf with the comment, "I will save that for the children." To me, for whom the rare sweet was a great treasure, Mother's act represented a supreme sacrifice and her self-denial and unselfishness left a deep impression upon my young mind.

Loyal always, loyal to her husband, her children, her friends! Is it to be wondered at that children reared in such homes should have memories that bind them with golden chains not only in grateful affection to their parents' memories, but to the principles for which such fathers and such mothers stood firm! Certain it is that when desperate sorrow came upon me, the recollection of my father's and my mother's faith in the righteousness of a Supreme Being was the deciding influence that carried my hesitating feet past the crossroads—past the place of despair.

On the day dedicated to the memory of our mothers—on the day when we wear the white carnation, so fittingly an emblem of our mothers' gracious lives, let us not only dwell with grateful affection upon our treasured memories but let us ponder, also, upon the influences which we are passing on to our children. Are we so living that our children may have recollections of our faith, our love, our courage, that will be as anchors to their souls when they, perhaps, are tempest-tossed and hard pressed by life's storms? All I ask for my children is that their memories may be as high and as fine as are mine of my father and my mother.

The Blessings Of Hardship

I HAVE sometimes referred to my experiences in the earlier years of business, not because of any desire to be retrospective, but in order that those who are just starting might be able to compare their own experiences with the hardships and sacrifices that were necessary for me to get a foothold.

And yet, I realize now they were never real hardships or sacrifices—rather they were open doors to future endeavors. I believe that few young couples are required to encounter more than my wife and I did in our early years. And yet I am thankful to God for those experiences, for I firmly believe we were guided by Him.

Courtesy

IF THE HISTORY of the unsuccessful businessmen of the world could be read, I believe that the element of discourtesy would be one of the contributing factors in their failure.

How often do we hear it said, "I do not like that proprietor, that manager, or that salesman." On the other hand, some people seem to radiate their wholesomeness. Their personality is pleasing, and without any thought of palaver, they are glad to see you and anxious to serve you.

The store which sells its wares for less but pays little attention to the service it renders does not meet with the success of the store with courteous employees. The public is not greatly interested in saving a little money on a purchase at the expense of service. Courteous treatment will make a customer a walking advertisement. A manager who has learned the value of courtesy will see that he has courteous clerks. He is cordial to his force and he demands the same treatment for his customers.

Where price alone is the drawing card, you will observe no degree of permanency in the clientele. In such stores, sales people are mere automatons who lack personal interest in the customer. The well-satisfied customer will bring the repeat sale that counts!

Intelligent Work

I BELIEVE in hard work as the prime solvent of life's problems. But misdirected work is wasted work, and youth needs the aid of wise counsel.

My father believed in work, but in labor with an intelligent purpose. I remember once in discussing the meaning of work with him, he told me how one of his early teachers asked him to shift a heap of stones from one side of the road to the other and then compelled him to lug them back again to teach him the importance of work as a moral discipline.

This is senseless instruction. It is the kind that makes ambitious young people rebel against memorizing lessons with no other apparent object than their purposeless repetition. Moral discipline that is not directed to useful results, like so-called mental discipline, that does not find satisfaction in significant achievement, destroys the finer fiber of youth.

Principle Or Profit?

SOON AFTER I went as a young man to the town of Longmont, about forty miles north of Denver, Colorado, I saw the notice of a shop for sale. It was a butcher shop. Having grown up on a stock farm it struck me that I could buy the stock—which would keep me outdoors, as the doctor had urged—and hire a man to look after the butchering.

I wrote my mother, telling her that it seemed the chance to go into business for myself and asking whether she could spare my savings of $300 so that I could take advantage of the opportunity. Without a word of doubt she sent the money.

I hurried to Longmont and bought the shop. The bold lettering of my name on the window served my vanity; a bull's head was painted over it, and "Meat Market" underneath. It may just be that there was something prophetic in my selection of the bull's head for the venture!

According to the butcher, who had had previous experience at that particular location, my success would depend heavily on the trade from the hotel. "To keep the hotel for a customer," he explained, "all you have to do is buy the chef a bottle of whisky a week."

At first I didn't give it much thought. I simply bought the whisky and gave it to the man. But I began remembering how my father, deeply aware of the havoc wrought in human lives by strong drink, had impressed the danger on the minds of his sons. Then it struck me forcibly that if he were alive he would be sadly disappointed, seeing me use whisky as a bribe for business gain. I made up my mind to buy the chef no more whisky, and never again to pursue profit in such a manner.

I explained to the chef, but the butcher had not exaggerated and I lost the trade of the hotel. Since it bulked so large in success or failure for the butcher shop, I lost that too and at the age of twenty-three I was flat broke. In my heart I knew it was right never to let go of a principle to hang onto a job. I did not regret taking the stand, but it was a costly lesson.

A Good Ending

THE ONLY THING I remember about my first day at school is a fight. Please understand that I have no pride in the memory, which is not very edifying. Indeed, I cannot tell now what it was all about. But, at any rate, I pitched head first into someone, bowled him over, and then ran for home. I know that I was not ordinarily belligerent and evidently I was very much provoked. I make no defense.

Oh, yes, I also remember that I was brought right back to school. That is, I am sure, the important thing. A bad beginning may be overcome by a good ending.

Why My Life Was Spared

I AM IN MY EIGHTIES. In the early summer of 1952, I suffered a collapse and was hospitalized with pneumonia. After a strenuous fight for my life in an oxygen tent, I learned that I had come back to the world. I realized how thin had been the thread connecting me with life when I heard that one wire service had even carried a report of my death. It was a shattering experience to be reminded that the greater part of my life is past.

Once on my feet again, I asked myself, "Why was I spared?" True, I still have much work planned—there are many things I want to do, and I dislike leaving tasks undone! But still I asked, "Why was I given another chance at life?"

I found at least one answer to my question when I received a telegram inviting me to speak on an interfaith program. An opportunity to accomplish one of the jobs I had yet to do—to be of service in promoting good faith among all peoples—was now mine. Do you think this is a sentimental attitude? Well, to me there can be no greater force for good than an interfaith spirit which moves across all lines of race, creed and color and, in so doing, announces to the world that all men are brothers.

How Experience Shows Itself

WHEN I ENTERED a store, upon the completion of my high school studies, I received a stipend of two dollars and twenty-seven cents a month. I continued to draw this salary for eleven months. When I applied for the position, the proprietor asked me, "What can you sell?"

"Oh," I said, "I know I can sell clothing."

A few days later one of my good friends came in for a suit of clothes. I shall never forget how deeply humiliated I was when I discovered I could not even sell my friend. But it was a splendid experience, for it took some of the conceit out of me. I began to study the different fabrics. I made all kinds of tests, in order to discover the differences between wool and cotton. I began to observe more closely the kind of goods that wear well and hold their shape. In fact, I made the clothing business a study, so that I could talk intelligently about clothes, and sell them.

VI
THE CHRISTIAN AND THE
SOCIAL ORDER

"Am I My Brother's Keeper?"

IT IS INTERESTING to recall that the man who first asked, "Am I my brother's keeper?" was not honestly seeking enlightenment, but disclaiming responsibility. He had done his brother irreparable harm and sought to hide his enormous guilt behind a mask of impertinence. Regardless of this, however, every time we meet this question *we are reminded of a relationship and an obligation.*

Cain's jeering reply to God's penetrating question reveals not only his sentiments toward his brother Abel, but also deep-seated contempt for his obligations.

In the light of this question, I invite you to think with me about a man who lived centuries later upon the plain of Esdraelon in the land of Palestine. Such was his faith and his obedience to God, so noble was his character, that today a great, nation-wide organization of traveling Christian laymen bears his name. Evil days had fallen upon the land and a mighty host of Midianites had descended upon the plain. Gideon knew what this meant to his people and his compassion was deeply stirred. Seeing this, God called him to the task of leading Israel against the enemy, and helped this man and three hundreds of his countrymen put the enemy to flight.

God is always making plans for the betterment, the uplift and the welfare of man. But the responsibility is not God's alone. History is the record of men's deeds and misdeeds as well as God's good works. Though I am convinced that there is a Divine purpose at work in the world, man must do his share toward the ultimate achievement of that purpose.

The Common Man

IN THE Bible story of Gideon we are impressed by the fact that *the three hundred men who stood with him about the enemy camp with trumpet and pitcher in hand were common men—not professional soldiers in any sense.* Some were tillers of the soil, others shepherds, and still others workmen in some trade. The world is filled with common men who go their quiet ways, turn the wheels of industry, produce crops, build our homes, and perform a multitude of everyday tasks. Geniuses are few and far between, only a few can be famous, and the rest of us must live our lives as just common people. We common folk are in the majority, which means that most of the work necessary to keep things going must be done by us.

Jesus honored the common man when He called the Twelve and assigned them an uncommon task. It is common people who found and maintain Christian homes, constitute the greater number of members of our churches, teach the thousands of Sunday-school classes every Sunday, and, without fanfare, recognition, and sometimes without praise, carry on the indispensable work of the Kingdom of Heaven. This, no doubt, fairly expresses the experience of most of you. The work which engages your interest and claims your time as churchmen is purely a work of love. You devote yourself to it, and maintain your church, for the sole reason that you feel the Man of Galilee has called you to share His tender, unselfish ministry.

The joy of being His yoke-fellow, and the deep, abiding satisfaction in rendering a service to your fellow men is your reward. It is a high privilege we have.

The Christian Way

WHEN I WAS a young man, it was generally accepted as a fact that a man could not create a fortune and remain a Christian. I wanted very much to do both. I believed it could be done. Looking back now upon that secret ambition of mine, I must admit the desire to become wealthy all but possessed my soul. When some progress was made, however, and because of my parents' influence and because my employer had given me such a wonderful opportunity to become independent, my interest shifted somewhat from my own self-interest to that of the men who worked with me. Their future became my concern.

As I grew and found myself faced with tragic disappointments which all must learn to face, there was something down underneath which was restless and unsatisfied. It was then I began my interest in philanthropic enterprises, churches, schools, hospitals and various charities.

May I mention one of these which has given me my greatest personal satisfaction? Some years ago in cooperation with Dr. Daniel A. Poling the idea of establishing a home for retired Christian workers was conceived. This was established in Florida, near Jacksonville. Some one hundred couples are able, after 40, 50 or 60 years of unselfish service in America or overseas, to live in quiet comfort and security. When I think of the prayers for peace emanating from that community home, I have been repaid a thousandfold for my investment.

Tolerance Of Our Fellow Man

I HAVE NO illusions about the power of mere words to persuade people to change their ways of thinking. But if I should succeed in reaching even one of you, I will at least have the comfort of having started a *chain* of faith and tolerance. For even a small light of faith can spread light to others. Not by what is said, but by behavior and attitude.

It is useless to say: "I love all men as my brothers," if we dislike and fear them in our hearts. We do *not* love our brothers if we say: "I love all men—excepting those who do not believe as I do." We do *not* love our brothers if we think: "I love all men—but that one I condemn because he is evil."

If we pass such judgment on others, we have not yet learned to love. And *there* is the crux of the problem—*there* is the great difficulty. I know how hard it is to be tolerant of people who are ruthless, greedy, selfish or who seem downright bad to us. It is very hard to love those who are unkind or cruel. It is more than difficult to think tolerantly of those who may be threatening the foundations of our democracy, a thing painfully built, and of great value to us. In brief, it is a great task to overcome our natural tendency to disapprove, suspect and dislike that which we do not understand.

Yet, being only human, we cannot understand everything, we cannot bring ourselves to love everybody. The great prophets and teachers and saints, they *did* understand, they

did have an all-embracing compassion. And certainly it is
something for which to strive. But if we cannot reach their
heights, we can at least tolerate. We can at least have faith in
our fellow man, in order to call forth his best impulses.

I have had many years of concrete and practical knowledge
of the way this works, and I know it to be true.

An All-Pervasive Rule

IN EVERY NORMAL human being there is an inherent disposition to defend the weak against the strong and to sympathize
with the downtrodden. The Golden Rule permeates our public and private justice and underlies all true religion.

For many hundred years after the Golden Rule fell from
the lips of the Master it was regarded as a beautiful idealism
rather than as a practical precept to be enacted in men's lives.
Its first application encompassed only the narrow scope of
friends and neighbors. Gradually, as horizons widened and
the definition of "brotherhood" took on a broader significance, the Golden Rule became a principle to be applied to
everyone with whom we came in contact.

Burden-bearers Of The Race

IT HAS BEEN my observation, and no doubt yours also, that *when need arises God always lays a burden upon somebody's heart and a task upon somebody's shoulders.* This is the simple story of achievement and progress. This was what happened with Moses, Gideon, the prophets, the twelve disciples, and most of all with the Son of God. To these might be added a long list of more modern men and women who, being aware of a great need, assumed a noble task.

Who has not heard of Father Damien, who at 33 volunteered for service in the Pacific Island leper colony? At a time when there was no organization, no sanitation, and little constructive activity for these unfortunates, Father Damien helped build houses, dug ditches for a water supply, alleviated suffering as much as possible. In due time hospitals were established, with resident doctors and nurses. After serving there fifteen years, Father Damien himself died a leper's death.

David Livingston did more to break up the slave trade in Africa than did any other man; Dr. Wilfred Grenfell spent his life in service to the people of Newfoundland and Labrador; Dr. Walter Reed threw his all into a battle to conquer yellow fever; crippled, suffering Louis Pasteur labored day and night in his laboratory, in spite of abuse and ridicule, to isolate the dread virus of hydrophobia. To these might be added scientists, teachers, philanthropists, businessmen—in fact, people both great and small from every walk and vocation in life. The human race has indeed been blessed with a glorious host of self-forgetful benefactors who found their chief joy in bearing the burdens of others.

He Did What He Could

IN THE TOWN of Gary, Indiana, so the story goes, Ethel Smith was badly burned. For days she lingered between life and death in the hospital. The physicians announced that the burn required an engraftment of skin before it would heal. Who would meet the demands of this unfortunate girl?

In that same town lived William Rugh, a crippled newsboy. When he learned the needs of the suffering girl, he offered his own skin to meet the demand. The operation was performed; but Ethel had to wait too long, and it was such an ordeal for William that he, too, died. Sad climax to such suffering and noble consecration. But in a sense, it was glorious. William did not know that Ethel had passed away, when just a few moments before he followed her into the life of rich reward, he said, "Well, I guess I am some good after all."

The whole world calls us to heal its blistering, festering sore. What greater task could we assume? What greater privilege could we desire? We have the chance to do "some good after all."

He Did What He Could

VII
THE AMERICAN WAY

The Privilege Of Being American

I AM CONCERNED, as I know you are, too, with the fact that
many of us are losing sight of what I call the main road of
American progress—the exercising of individual initiative,
the assuming of individual responsibility. We have let ourselves stray a long way on a side road, by gradually, almost
imperceptibly, relinquishing our privilege to do a job for
ourselves.

Maybe it seems strange to you, my using the word "privilege" in such a sense. Privilege, to most people, means some-
thing-for-nothing, an unearned advantage. I use "privilege"
in the sense of opportunity to fulfill one's destiny, to increase
one's stature as a human being, to produce. That is what I
call our special American privilege. And that is the one we
must fight to keep.

If every one of us reading these lines should resolve that,
from this day forward, he would be the master of his own
life as an American individual—if every one of us should
resolve he would let no opportunity pass to assert his independent right to remain free—that would be a big step
forward.

One way we have done less than our best is with our young
people. These young Americans are today better housed,
better clothed, better educated than ever before in history.
But we have not shown them clearly enough how great a
privilege it is to be an American—we have not made them
understand the character-building virtues of depending on
their own effort and determination.

Character Is Ours To Develop

THIS NATION has often been compared to a pendulum which suffers its swings of public opinion from one extreme to another, but whose resultant course is one balance. However, to achieve that goal of national balance, we must first achieve it among the majority of our individual citizens. Let us consider then what we can do to help the individual, and what better place to start than with the young boy or girl who is still malleable enough in his ideals and outlook to profit from sound guidance given in the spirit of helpfulness.

Such a subject should deal fundamentally with the formation of character. No man is born with character, which may be defined as the quality of leadership, or the ability to do great things. It is rather a product of one's development throughout the years. The next time you see a person you greatly admire, I invite you to look back over his history. You will find that he is just like you in that he made mistakes, he had fears, he worried at times, and he often became discouraged. But while some people rise above their problems and overcome them, others become submerged by them.

A Dream Always Coming True

IN HIS BOOK, *The Christ of the American Road,* E. Stanley Jones says, "America is a dream unfulfilled." If America is an unfulfilled dream, it is the business of all who teach the young to lead them forward in the grand work of fulfillment. By this I mean all upon whom the responsibility for teaching falls—parents, teachers, ministers, businessmen, statesmen and others. In this day when a veritable Pandora's box of isms has been let loose upon a long-suffering world, we must give more earnest heed to the most precious treasure ever bestowed upon mankind—Americanism! And what is Americanism? Professor Orton, in his *America in Search of a Culture,* comes close to defining it when he says the American tradition "is a dauntless faith in ends that are ever renewed, and in the power of ordinary human beings to attain those ends. It bids us try this means and that means and the other means with our eyes fixed upon the goal, and try and fail, and try again, and in the end get there." Americanism, then, is a dream which is always coming true—a tradition which goes before like a pillar of cloud by day and of fire by night.

The Path Before Us

WE ARE TODAY the world's greatest nation. We're the might-
iest. We're the wealthiest. Yet we are not the first in history to
attain that top spot among the nations of the world. One
nation after another has made the long struggle upward, stood
for a period of time, some longer than others, on the pinnacle
of national greatness and power, and disappeared down the
other side.

Some of those nations we have with us yet. Others are not
more than mummified relics on the desert of time! Some of
these nations are today no more than names in the history
books. It's important that we of the United States keep this
in mind. This power which is ours today is not necessarily
permanent. This wealth is not necessarily enduring. It can
disappear within the lifetime of some of those who read these
lines. We are in the second half of the twentieth century—
and when this century dawned, old England was on top. The
British fleet ruled the waves. Men said that the sun never set
on British soil. The pound sterling controlled the economy
of the world.

Because we hold today the position England held fifty
years ago, the position so many other nations held before
her, it behooves us that we ask ourselves where we'll be fifty
years from now—at this century's end. That answer will be
found to be spiritual as well as industrial, moral as well as
economic. "What shall it profit a man if he gain the whole

world and lose his own soul?" Jesus asked. That question is for nations as well as for individuals. Neither men nor nations can live by physical bread *alone*.

Personal Organization

No MAN MAY reasonably expect to become a success unless he has his forces properly marshalled and working in perfect harmony. He must fix his ideal and then apply organized principles to himself, his habits and conduct, in order to attain his purpose.

This personal organization will come about when men willingly put themselves under severe training, and under the steady hand of self-government. A man applying the principles of his business to himself would work out an ideal for and with his family as a group, for his children as individuals, and for himself as a responsible guide. He would never be conquered by money nor by material possessions, but would govern them wisely.

In this self-organization, a man should be encouraged to think of himself in relation to the larger things of life. All his life should be the Golden Rule in active application toward God, fellow man, community, family and business.

Faith In America

NOTHING HAS EVER shaken my faith in America and in the American way of life. I believe that this country is the greatest country on earth, but I am more concerned that it should be the best. I believe in American freedom and democracy, and I want freedom and democracy to increase. I want its benefits and opportunities to reach into every section of the land, into every group, into every home and to the last man, woman and child. I believe that what we have under our flag and what we are striving to achieve has been divinely ordained and that God has an even greater mission for America among the nations of the world.

The United States was founded in prayer, in faith and in the spirit of sacrifice. Our God-fearing Founding Fathers were ready to lay down their lives for freedom to worship God according to the dictates of their own consciences. They even made the supreme sacrifice upon fields of battle to support their beliefs and to pass freedom on to their children and their children's children.

So far as the future is concerned, our national fate will be determined by our choice of the hard right rather than the easy wrong. Spiritual as well as physical muscles become flabby when they are not exercised. Dr. Ira Landreth, a former president of Ward-Belmont College in Nashville, Tennessee, once said: "*We need moral muscles for mighty tasks.*" Neither men nor nations develop muscles adequate for

mighty tasks unless they use them. Let us choose the hard
right. This will be our daily contribution in helping to make
America strong.

America's Creed

ONCE AGAIN, the nation in reflective mood should gather
about our shrines and in our sanctuaries of sacred freedom to
pledge anew its devotion to those inalienable rights and liber-
ties for which the sword of Cornwallis was demanded. Once
again the nation would do well to bare its head, bend its knee
and in unison repeat the American Creed:

"I believe in the United States of America as a government of the people, by the people, for the people, whose just
powers are derived from the consent of the governed; a
democracy in a republic; a sovereign nation of many sovereign
states; a perfect union, one and inseparable; established upon
those principles of freedom, equality, justice and humanity
for which American patriots sacrificed their lives and fortunes. I, therefore, believe it is my duty to my country to love
it, to support its Constitution, to obey its laws, to respect its
flag, and to defend it against all enemies."

Covenant For Americans

FELLOW AMERICANS, let us get back to fundamentals, to the place where we recognize that something for nothing is as morally reprehensible as it is economically unsound and unsafe. Let us each shoulder his share of the responsibility for strengthening the moral and spiritual life of America.

The dark clouds of Communism are settling over the East and even rolling in over Europe. Our foreign commitments are heavy and the dangers of war are great. But if we, the American people, are to play our historic role in this 20th century, we must first of all be internally sound. Except we are internally sound, we can never be externally great. Except we're economically solvent, we can't possibly be, over any protracted period of time, militarily strong. And our moral and spiritual strength must have sound industrial, economic and social foundations. Nor can we fight Communism as an ideology except we can show to the peoples of the world that we have something finer, better and infinitely greater here in America.

A present trend has to be reversed. The "something for nothing" idea must be repudiated. Public opinion has to be changed, or we shall lose for ourselves and our children every good and wholesome thing we cherish. Let's be up and about the supreme business of being free Americans. Let us recognize the dangers that are about us and the opportunity that is before us. Let us see the full glory of "this last best hope of earth," and accepting responsibility as our fathers did at the nation's birth, let us covenant together, humbly and sincerely "pledging ourselves, our lives, our fortunes and our sacred honor" to the cause of a free and greater America.

Loyalty To God And Man

A MAN WHO is not loyal to his country is a traitor. Such a man is dealt with harshly, and it is right that he should be, for what kind of government would we have were we to allow men to malign it? I sometimes think that disloyalty is a result of ignorance. No one of ordinary intelligence would bite the hand that feeds him. How few of us really appreciate what is done for us. How liable we are to forget, after we have reached an advanced position in life, the helping hand that piloted us through on the start. A man can be disloyal to God, though he may receive no physical punishment unless he commits some act that is in defiance of the law. Yet he is punished just as surely, for compensation is inevitable.

I never expect to see a paradise on this earth; but if men would be thoroughly unselfish and loyal to one another, we should then approach a degree of perfection that has not yet been attained.

The Genius Of America

WHY TODAY's apparent dread of hard work on the part of so many young people—and older people, too?

Why this snobbery that considers it more honorable to pick up a telephone than to pick up a shovel?

Why this contempt for productive work?

George Washington was a surveyor; Paul Revere was a silversmith; Abraham Lincoln was a country storekeeper; Benjamin Franklin was a printer and an electrician—in fact, the best electrician of his time; Thomas Jefferson was a designer. I could put together quite a list of such people. They all used their hands.

Years ago, a young man named Earl Corder Sams came from Simpson, Kansas, to Kemmerer, Wyoming, to work in my first store. He waited on customers, swept and scrubbed floors, washed windows, kept the stock clean and, when I was absent, milked the family cow. His hours were from 7 o'clock in the morning until 10 or 11 o'clock at night. His pay was $75 a month.

After a year in Kemmerer, he went to Cumberland, Wyoming, to manage his first store. There he was the boss. He did not have to milk a cow, but together with his wife, he did all the work in the store, in addition to hauling his water supply from a creek half a mile distant. Together they were paid a salary of $1,500 a year. He was one of my first partners. He became president, and then chairman, of the Penney Company.

I say that the genius of America is not in the arts.

The genius of America is in doing things—making things!

The Honest Workman

THE LABORER who loafs on his job is just as guilty as the merchant who gives short count or who advertises falsely.

The man in business who makes business solely the means to a selfish end is hopeless. He is too busy making and spending money to give much thought to his less fortunate neighbors. He oftentimes is unmindful of the obligation he owes. He accepts the benefits afforded by our democratic form of government as if they were his heritage without obligation. It is a personal misfortune to have no higher ideal than the amassing of a fortune. The more such a man gets the more he wants, and as his wealth increases, his desires increase.

When a man can afford it, he should have, within reason, that which his heart desires; but it is nothing short of criminal for a man to spend money on himself alone, with no concern whatever for those worthy of his aid and assistance.

Salesmen Of Freedom

WHY DOES America have the world's highest standard of living? We do not have greater natural resources such as coal and iron and timber than other nations, as so many seem to think. There are other nations such as Russia and China and India which have these samples of national wealth in greater abundance than we do. But we have more conveniences than any other people—and this I emphasize:

Because we are a free people—

We are free to make and to sell; to buy and to save; to be farmers or machinists, merchants, doctors or lawyers; free to speak out, free to worship as we choose, free to come and free to go in an economy embedded in the principle of example rather than in the gloom of envy.

If we were good salesmen of freedom, do you suppose Communism would have been able to overrun half the world in less than a generation?

If we were good salesmen of freedom, do you suppose Communism would have been able to cross our own borders and penetrate our schools, our churches, our government, our homes?

Do you suppose, if we really believed in freedom, half of the world would be hating us, and the remaining half distrusting us?

You might think about those things. In fact, if you love

this land and its freedom, it is imperative for you to think about them. Imperative that we—you and I—do something about it. It is of highest importance that we subscribe again to that American principle known as self-reliance—believe again in its promise that any man's success indicates what every man can do, if he tries.

Principles Of Successful Business

I HAVE SEEN the ambitious prosper and ventures thrive. I have seen aspirants fall and businesses fail during my lifetime. Invariably it has been the persons of commendable character who have succeeded permanently and those of unworthy principles who have failed, even though temporary success was theirs. The former, knowingly or unknowingly, practiced Biblical precepts; the latter did not. When I say the Bible I mean the principles it stands for: integrity, humility, diligence, charity, and patience.

History proves that the greatest men and kingdoms have been the humblest, that nothing succeeds like honesty, that there is no substitute for labor, that patience builds and impatience wrecks, and that charity has sweet fruits.

America Is Your Responsibility

We need to recognize that if this magnificent thing which men call the American Way of Life shall pass away, or be unalterably changed, *history will not hold us guiltless*. We must not, we cannot fail to accept the responsibilities which our free society places upon us. What are we doing individually and personally? We need to become informed concerning the principles of sound economics. It's not enough to say the taxes are too high, or that the welfare state is too costly, or that bureaucracy is inherently inefficient. We need to understand clearly the function of capital—as well as that of labor.

Let us lose no opportunity in our personal contacts or through our businesses, and most of all in our association with our own employees, to disseminate the facts concerning our economy.

Let us lose no opportunity to exert every influence we have and can muster politically, and be active in the party of our individual allegiance.

Let us rally to our side every public opinion-molding force which we can influence. Let us make certain that our clergy, those who minister to us and to our families and speak from our pulpits, know the basic facts of sound economics.

Let us conduct ourselves and our businesses with a strict sense of personal morality and social responsibility. Let us give every man his due and do it voluntarily.

Finally, and most important of all, let us do everything in our power to strengthen those institutions out of which has grown this philosophy which created America, the American home and the American church. Character develops in the home. And the social attitudes so important to a free society are more often *caught* than *taught,* and they are caught from the child's parents most easily and most often.

As regards the church: make no mistake about it, the American Way of Life is a by-product of man's faith in the Fatherhood of God, and the brotherhood of all mankind.

Patriotism

AN OLD AXIOM reads, "Where the heart is right, there is true patriotism." The real patriot respects law and order and does his duty toward his country and his fellow men.

A patriot is one who loves his country and ever seeks to act in defense of it. A country is its people, institutions, and ideals for which our forefathers fought that we might have political, educational and religious freedom.

Acting in defense of one's country does not mean resistance only when its institutions are assailed. It means upholding it at all times. Every man is by his actions either upholding American institutions or unconsciously undermining them.

America Is No Accident!

THERE ARE SUPERFICIAL thinkers—some of whom call themselves "economists," who tell us, and much more important, *teach* our children—that the wealth and power of America is merely the result of fortuitous circumstance: that it happened our pioneer forefathers stumbled on a virgin continent and that we, the American people, have done no more than exploit its natural resources. This is sheerest nonsense.

We do have natural resources of course, but many another nation has had, and *has,* far more in natural resources and has had more time to develop them. *No, America is more than a lucky accident.*

Is it that our people work harder than the other peoples of the earth? There one comes near to the answer, for our forefathers started out holding no more than a beachhead on the edge of a vast, wild, unbroken continent—from which they had to literally *hew* and *dig* and *build* this mighty nation. But hard work is not the only answer. Men everywhere—Chinese coolies, Russian serfs, Italian peasants—have worked from time immemorial. *No, it has taken something more than work to make America.*

Perhaps the answer is that we are a breed apart? That we have more brains, greater intelligence? Again the answer is not satisfying. Our forefathers came from a score of European countries where they endured the same hardships, suffered the same privations, knew the same indignities as those who remained there. *It's not solely a question of gray matter.*

What is it then? Let us go back to that core-hard question of our national greatness. A part of the answer lies here: *In the American way of life there has been from the very beginning, an incentive for a man to work.* There was an incentive to work because there was *an incentive to save;* there was the incentive to save because there was *an incentive to invest.* America is the result of *natural resources* plus *labor* plus *invested capital.* America today has the power that it has, and the American people today enjoy the living standard which they have, because under private ownership and with the incentive of free enterprise, in open competition, *the American people produce more than any other people in any other nation of the world.*

The Past Points The Way

THE HIGHEST CALLING in life for any of us, save that of being a humble follower of God, is that of being like the Americans of bygone days who developed this country and made it what it is. James Truslow Adams tells in his *Epic of America* what has always been the American dream—a vision of society in which the lot of the common man will be easier, a dream of richer, better and happier life for all the citizens of every rank. This was the dream which set the faces of the Pilgrims toward the New World in 1620, inspired the Declaration of Independence in 1776, under whose aegis the Constitution was formed in 1787, and which irresistibly led the people westward across mountain range and desert to the golden sands of the Pacific Ocean.

America Has Been Good To Me

TODAY I REMEMBER that the years have rewarded me for every talent I possess, and for every effort I've ever made—amply rewarded me not only with the world's material goods, but richly rewarded me in many, many fine friendships—rewarded me too with an almost endless series of deep and gratifying experiences.

This is no casual thought. I have often pondered it. I write of this now not merely because America has been good to me. It's often difficult for us of the United States to see this. Most of us were born in this country; we grew up here. Without giving it any particular thought we accept our country and the vast wealth, the many advantages, and the countless opportunities which it so lavishly bestows upon us. *We take America for granted.*

But while this may be quite natural—and is certainly understandable—it's also dangerous. "Those to whom much is given, from them much shall be required." This ancient precept is as true for us today as it was for those to whom it was originally addressed two thousand years ago. Sometimes we forget that those stern old statements so cardinal in the faith of our fathers are true, not because they are written in the Scriptures, but rather they are written in the Scriptures because they're true.

Thanksgiving

THANKSGIVING IS ONE of America's outstanding annual festival days. Our Pilgrim Fathers first observed it at Plymouth in 1621 as an occasion to express their gratitude to God for His many mercies.

Two vitally constructive elements were manifest in the Thanksgiving attitude of the Pilgrims: they assembled for worship, thus recognizing God as the Blesser of their labors and the Giver of all good things; and they placed great emphasis on the instruction of their youth, thus acknowledging education as one of the principal factors in the attainment of life's largest possibilities.

These two elements—worship and education—have possessed the mind and heart of America's increasing population. There is no creed or cult recognizing the Fatherhood of God and His approval of the honest efforts of men, in our knowledge, that does not participate in the American spirit of Thanksgiving. We all ought, once a year, to spend one day in devout recognition of our Heavenly Father, who has blessed the Nation with bountiful crops and prosperity.

Opportunity—A Part Of Freedom

TODAY WE HAVE neither time nor money to spend on those who do not support Freedom.

In an economy where men are free, the doors are always open, the shelves always well stocked, the goods always priced right.

But, for too long a time, we have been trusting strangers to watch the shelves and to price the merchandise. Instead of being the merchants, we have been the customers—and I think you will agree we have bought some pretty expensive gadgets these years.

To pay for them we are going to have to put all our productive forces to work; and we are going to have to keep them working as far into the future as any of us can see. Not only that, but we are going to have to be frugal—in the management of our homes, our businesses and our government. We simply cannot—*must not!*—fail in our efforts to keep our freedoms.

We are not only the world's best hope of free men.

We are its *last* hope!

If, as a people, we expect to remain free, we will have to concentrate on three things: Opportunity. Work. Selling.

Let's consider opportunity first:

Three centuries ago, and more, the Pilgrims came to this country in search of economic opportunity—as well as to further religious freedom—something the Pilgrims already had won, as a reading of Governor William Bradford's *History of Plymouth Plantation* will show.

Coming here, the Pilgrims learned that economic opportunity required more of them than they required of it. They found it required of them that they be builders—builders of a nation that would serve not just them, as free men, but a nation that would serve *all*—all who came with them, all who came after them.

They learned there are no halfway resting places in opportunity. They found that where there is opportunity the way to arrive is to keep going. That is what we—you and I—must do. We must keep going—no matter what our disposition to stop and rest, no matter what the hardships and sacrifices, in the building of this nation, the United States of America.

Men Do Not Stand Still

SUCCESS CANNOT come from standstill men. Methods change and men must change with them. Methods change when the awkward process gives way to the congenial and direct. Men change when they drop habits that impede them and take on new ones that give them more skill, greater speed, and clearer vision.

Therefore, into modern business has come the idea of education, and of keeping men thoroughly informed about the ideals of the business. They are shown how to construct for themselves that subtle thing called character so that it will serve them and the business more efficiently.

The Way To Greatness

WHY DO THE American people produce more than any people
in any other nation of the world? Does the American work
harder? *He doesn't work as hard.* Does the American work
longer hours? *He doesn't work as long.* Does the American
laboring man work for less? *The American laboring man gets
far more.*

How is it then that the individual American produces
more than the individual Italian or Frenchman or English-
man or Russian? The answer of course is that the American's
money is invested in mechanical aids one thousand times
stronger and in some cases a hundred thousand times faster
than his own arm, or eye, or brain.

One of the problems of England today lies in the fact that
the present British government is living beyond its income.
But there is another problem just as deep and just as vital, in
the British economy. An American worker in pig iron accomplishes *four times* as much for every man-hour he puts in as
does his British counterpart. The American worker making
automobile tires accomplishes three times as much per man-
hour as does his British counterpart. Compare the American
worker with his British cousin, industry for industry, and *the
American worker accomplishes three times as much as the
Britisher for every hour put in.*

The reasons for this go back a bit: In 1929 Britain was turning back, percentage-wise of her national income, for the
modernization and maintenance of her industrial plant, only
two-thirds of what she had been turning back twenty years
before. In 1929 American industry was plowing back for

the same purpose, *50 per cent* more than it had been turning
back twenty years before.

I bring these facts to your attention because over certain
areas of America I detect an increasingly accepted belief that
somehow a nation can *legislate* its way into national greatness
and national prosperity. Increasingly men accept the belief
that a government *can* and *should* guarantee its citizens economic security and prosperity. France traveled this road after
World War I. England is trying it today. It has carried countless nations to the edge of the abyss—and over. Today we in
our wealth are supporting them in their bankruptcy while we
are tempted to pursue the same dangerous course. What is
the answer?

Character In Business

MANY A MAN has been confronted with serious personal business problems, and his decision, if fortunate, has been based
on some teaching from the Bible, although he may not say so.
More and more the influence of this Book is being felt in the
commercial world.

If an applicant for a position has a good character recom-
mendation—and most employers demand such of their help—
it is tantamount to saying the applicant possesses Christian
attributes of character. I know that in the firms I am connected with, emphasis is placed on character requisites that
are deemed paramount for the immortal life.

America's Destiny

As LONG AS we have faith at all in God, we must know that He is all-powerful, that His will for the world is justice and right and that eventually His purpose will be established here on earth. Good emerges slowly, but we must not doubt its final victory.

These are my convictions as to the world aspect in its relation to an overruling Providence.

As to our country, my faith in our America, in its people and in its way of life is unwavering. I believe its founding was divinely ordained, and that God has a mighty mission for it among the nations of the world.

America was founded in prayer, in faith and in the heroic spirit of sacrifice. Lives of comparative ease in their own countries might have been our forefathers' had they been willing to surrender their convictions. But they were ready to lay down their lives for freedom to worship God according to the dictates of their consciences. They underwent grievous hardships—many did lay down their lives—and throughout the nation's history, when the occasion has made necessary, their descendants have paid the supreme sacrifice upon its battlefield to preserve these principles of freedom.

In the immortal words of Lincoln: "It is rather for us to be here dedicated to the great task before us . . . that this nation, under God, shall have a new birth of freedom—and that Government of the people, by the people, for the people, shall not perish from the earth."